GROWING TOGETHER

Insights and Practices for Raising Faithful Kids

Denise Janssen,
Carmichael D. Crutchfield,
Virginia A. Lee, and
Jessica Young Brown,
Editors

Afterword by Patrick B. Reyes

Judson Press™
DISTINGUISHED PUBLISHERS SINCE 1824
VALLEY FORGE, PA

Growing Together: Insights and Practices for Raising Faithful Kids
© 2025 by Judson Press, Valley Forge, PA 19482-0851
All rights reserved.

No part of this publication may be reproduced, stored in a retrieval system, or transmitted in any form or by any means, electronic, mechanical, photocopying, recording, or otherwise, without the prior permission of the copyright owner, except for brief quotations included in a review of the book.

No part of this book may be used or reproduced in any manner for the purpose of training artificial intelligence technologies or systems, including but not limited to machine learning models, generative artificial intelligence, large language models (LLMs) or any derivative right in or to the Work not mentioned above, whether now known or hereafter devised.

Judson Press has made every effort to trace the ownership of all quotes. In the event of a question arising from the use of a quote, we regret any error made and will be pleased to make the necessary correction in future printings and editions of this book.

Bible quotations in this volume are from New Revised Standard Version, Updated Edition. Copyright © 2021 National Council of Churches of Christ in the United States of America. Used by permission. All rights reserved worldwide. Also Scripture quotations marked (NIV) are taken from the Holy Bible, New International Version®, NIV®. Copyright © 1973, 1978, 1984, 2011 by Biblica, Inc.™ Used by permission of Zondervan. All rights reserved worldwide. www.zondervan.com.The "NIV" and "New International Version" are trademarks registered in the United States Patent and Trademark Office by Biblica, Inc.™

Interior design by Crystal Devine.
Cover design by Lisa Cain.

Library of Congress Cataloging-in-Publication data

Names: Janssen, Denise editor | Crutchfield, Carmichael editor | Lee, Virginia (Virginia J.) editor | Brown, Jessica Young editor
Title: Growing together : insights and practices for raising faithful kids / Denise Janssen, Carmichael D Crutchfield, Virginia Lee, Jessica Young Brown, [editors].
Description: First. | Valley Forge, PA : Judson Press, [2025]
Identifiers: LCCN 2024051488 (print) | LCCN 2024051489 (ebook) | ISBN 9780817018504 trade paperback | ISBN 9780817082574 epub
Subjects: LCSH: Church work with children | Child rearing--Religious aspects--Christianity | Parenting--Religious aspects--Christianity
Classification: LCC BV639.C4 G77 2025 (print) | LCC BV639.C4 (ebook) | DDC 268/.432--dc23/eng/20250326
LC record available at https://lccn.loc.gov/2024051488
LC ebook record available at https://lccn.loc.gov/2024051489

Printed in the U.S.A.

First printing, 2025.

Contents

Setting the Stage

Introduction................................... 3

Christian Parenting as a Practice of Hospitality:
Love, Listening, Learning, Limits.................... 9
Peter Gathje

"But Why?"..................................... 22
Emily A. Peck

Section I: Good Roots: Caregiver Practices to Build a Foundation of Faith

1. "Let the Children Come": One Church's Story of Congregational Transformation............. 33
   Mary Young
2. Children's Bibles and Your Child............... 43
   Russell W. Dalton
3. Choosing Books for Children.................. 54
   Virginia A. Lee
4. Keeping the End in Mind..................... 65
   Denise Janssen
5. "And I Am Way More"....................... 75
   Tamar Wasoian

Section II: The Sticky Stuff: Caregiver Practices in Times of Challenge

6. Nurturing Faith through Intergenerational Storytelling and Play......................... 91
   G. Lee Ramsey Jr. and Mary Leslie Dawson-Ramsey
7. The Spirituality of Grand*parenting: When Grandparents Become Primary Caregivers...... 102
   Teresa E. Jefferson-Snorton

8. Fostering Resilient Children: Insights from a
   Freirean Approach 114
   Débora B. Agra Junker
9. Dreaming in the Valley of Dry Bones:
   Childcare and Advocacy for the Undocumented
   Children in the United States 129
   Heesung Hwang

Section III: In Search of Freedom: Caregiver Practices to Support Justice at Home and in the World

10. Young, Gifted, and Black 143
    Barbara Fears
11. The Dancing Mind of Parenting 152
    Zanique Davis
12. Mentoring with Intentionality and Purpose:
    A Necessity in Caregiving for African American
    Adolescent Males 164
    Carmichael D. Crutchfield
13. Conscious Parenting as Liberative Parenting 179
    Jessica Young Brown
14. Reflective Practice for Sexual Formation 190
    Margaret Conley
15. All Children Are a Part of the Village:
    Neurodivergence in Communities of Faith 208
    Timothy Lucas

Afterword: Growing Together 220
Patrick B. Reyes

Biographical Snapshots of the Contributors of
Reflections in this Book 229

Setting the Stage

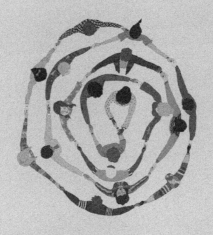

Introduction

Faith formation is sometimes considered a task that parents and caregivers delegate to the church, but this has not always been the case. Throughout history, families have played a central role in the faith formation of the next generation. When a congregation was involved, it was typically as the center for corporate worship, which engaged the whole gathered community across all ages and stages. With the emergence of the Sunday school movement in the eighteenth century in the United States, a distinct and focused time emerged in the context of the congregation for teaching and learning, primarily to expand literacy and instill a solid work ethic. By the end of the nineteenth century, the idea of teaching the tenets of the faith in age-specific groupings, much as public schools taught "reading, writing, and arithmetic" in graded classrooms, became the norm in mainline Christianity. The church's role, taking the lead in Christian faith formation, became the norm for most of the twentieth century and into the twenty-first. This gave rise to a professional approach to Christian education.

While professionalizing Christian faith formation has had its benefits, it fostered a false sense that parents and caregivers were ancillary to the faith development of their children. Perhaps the "leave it to the professionals" message left parents and caregivers feeling like their impact was minimal and their input was not required. However, research consistently shows this is not the case—children's faith is impacted more deeply by their experiences with parents and caregivers than any other source. Now we are beginning to see a movement emerging in the post-pandemic culture to encourage and equip parents and caregivers to take a greater role and responsibility in their children's faith development. And so we created this resource to equip parents and caregivers with accessible information drawn from scholarship to help them reflect on and engage in their role as their children's primary religious educators and for congregations to engage in conversations with parents and caregivers.

In the first book in this series, *Raising Faithful Kids: This is the Stuff of Faith*, various diverse authors helped us to read, think, reflect, and pray about the "real stuff" of life that contributes to faith.[1] We noted all the opportunities that occur within families for children and their adults to have conversations about important matters. We highlighted the importance of openness and curiosity on the part of children and adults. And we recognized that caregivers include stepparents, foster parents, aunts and uncles, grandparents, godparents, and other adults who love and care for children.

This volume aims to help you discern what it looks like to put theory into practice. We asked scholars in religious and theological education to reflect on their own experiences as parents and caregivers and to infuse theory into those reflections. Their assertions are not necessarily prescriptive, but they invite you to think about how theory can inform your practices, both in your personal caregiving and in congregational life. The reflections span the full gamut of human experience: tough age ranges, unexpected caregiving responsibilities, sexual health, and how to support kids who face added struggles of various forms. Ultimately, we want you to reflect on each chapter in a place of wondering: How could I implement these practices (or ones like these) in my own caregiving or in the context of my congregation?

We hope these chapters give you a starting point from which you can explore affirming and inclusive ways to support, encourage, and challenge the children in your life. While you might notice that some chapters seem to focus on certain ethnic, racial, or cultural groups, this does not mean those chapters are irrelevant to your caregiving. Each chapter possesses lessons for all of us to learn regardless of our specific cultural context. The organization of this book does not require that you approach it linearly, though we believe there is a sound logic to the order and groupings of the chapters. You are encouraged to move around the volume and pay special attention to the offerings that pique your interest. However, we encourage you to read this introduction in conjunction with the first two chapters. We believe these reflections will help you develop a helpful stance with which to approach the book. "Christian Parenting as a Practice of Hospitality" by Peter Gathje and "But Why?" by Emily Peck offer an emotional and mental foundation that you will see mirrored in the rest of the chapters.

A primary task of this work is to invite you to think about the attitude with which you approach caregiving. Faith formation is not simply a task assigned to adults. It is a product of rich, intentional relationships that adapt as children grow and develop. We hope that Gathje's and Peck's offerings will invite you into some self-reflection that will be critical for the path forward and help you to realistically discern next steps from the more content-oriented chapters that follow. We know that while faith formation can happen in dyads between kids and caregivers, it also happens in the context of community. We hope that entire faith communities will engage this resource as a way to reflect on our communal faith formation practices and the extent to which they accomplish the goal of helping children navigate their faith in more personalized and long-lasting ways. To this end, each chapter concludes with a list of discussion questions that can be pondered personally and in community. These questions are framed to help congregations discern ways to more fully support children's faith formation based on logistical, financial, and cultural realities. We know that not every family or congregation is called to act in the same way. But we also know that every family or congregation is called to act in some way. We hope that this resource is a tool to help you figure out your way.

In the first of two chapters in the introductory section, Peter Gathje draws connections between the biblical and Christian traditions of hospitality and how that might help us develop practices of love, listening, learning, and limits with children. In the second chapter, Emily A. Peck invites us to wonder alongside our children about our faith. Adults do not have to know all the answers!

In Section One, which is about "Good Roots," the authors explore some practices that help to build a foundation for our faith. Mary Young provides an example of what can happen when a congregation truly welcomes children by listening and learning from them, and by receiving the gifts that the children offered to the community. Recognizing the many choices available, Russell W. Dalton provides an insightful and helpful perspective on evaluating and choosing children's Bibles. Since books are a way in which children learn about themselves and the world, Virginia A. Lee helps adults think about the books they choose for children and what they might represent. Denise Janssen draws our attention to thinking about what we want to achieve in our parenting and caregiving practices and then considers how we might go about it. Tamar Wasoian provides new insight into developmental theory and neuroscience and how they influence how we understand children and faith.

In Section Two, titled "The Sticky Stuff," the authors consider faith practices during times of challenge. G. Lee Ramsey Jr. and Mary Leslie Dawson-Ramsey provide an example of how one community engaged in intergenerational storytelling during a global pandemic. Teresa E. Jefferson-Snorton challenges congregations to consider how to support children and caregivers in a variety of family configurations, especially ones in which grandparents are primary caregivers.

Débora B. Agra Junker calls us to consider how the concept of integrating theory and action as proposed by educator Paulo Freire can offer insight for fostering faith. Heesung Hwang provides biblical and theological foundations, along with practical resources for how faith communities can be places of hospitality, welcome, and justice for immigrant children.

In Section Three, "In Search of Freedom," the authors explore practices that support justice. Barbara Fears explores culturally relevant pedagogy and its importance for Black students. Zanique Davis considers what it means to nurture a flourishing faith identity with an emphasis on what flourishing means. Carmichael D. Crutchfield shares learnings from a mentoring program and its importance for African American adolescent males. In her discussion of conscious parenting, Jessica Young Brown provides the reasons for and the results of a liberative, justice-seeking way of parenting. In her chapter, Margaret Conley describes a way in which parents, caregivers, and faith communities might employ reflective conversations about sexuality and sexual formation. Timothy Lucas asks faith communities to consider their role in welcoming neurodivergent children and receiving their gifts.

We hope these authors provide helpful information, new insights, affirmations, and challenges for all parents, caregivers, and faith communities. Welcoming children with hospitality and helping them engage their faith with wonder and curiosity is a sacred calling for all followers of Jesus.

Note

1. Denise Janssen, Carmichael Crutchfield, Virginia A. Lee, and Jessica Young Brown, eds., *Raising Faithful Kids: This Is the Stuff of Faith* (Valley Forge, PA: Judson Press, 2024).

Christian Parenting as a Practice of Hospitality: Love, Listening, Learning, Limits

PETER GATHJE

When we become parents, we welcome a stranger into our midst. We are suddenly responsible for a person who is new to our home and our family. For some this idea may seem like a bucket of cold water thrown on the joy of becoming a parent. For others this may seem like a realistic assessment of parenthood. In this chapter, I draw on the Christian tradition of hospitality toward strangers as a resource for Christian parenting. I see four practices within Christian hospitality that may inform our practice of Christian parenting: love, listening, learning, and limits.

I begin with the story of Abraham and Sarah, who offer hospitality and are graciously gifted with a child in their old age (Genesis 18:1-15). This paradigmatic story shows not only the hospitable welcome of strangers but also how hospitality (like parenting) is mutually transformative. In offering hospitality, the hosts also receive precious gifts from their guests.

Three angels disguised as men arrive at Abram and Sarai's tent. Abram and Sarai quickly go to work to serve the strangers. In response the strangers promise that when they return, Abram and Sarai will have a child. Sarai laughs (in another version of the story, Abram laughs, too; see Genesis 17:17). But God and the angels have the final laugh. Abram and Sarai become parents at the ripe old ages of one hundred and ninety, respectively. In fact a shift in their roles is accompanied by a shift in their names, as they become Abraham and Sarah.

This story is intimately tied to how I see a connection between hospitality and parenting. In offering hospitality, I became a father. For nearly twenty years, my wife, Kathleen, and I have provided hospitality to people on the streets at Manna House in Memphis, Tennessee. Manna House offers those in homelessness and/or poverty a safe space, showers, clothing, and coffee in an atmosphere of respect for the dignity of each person. Like in the story of Abraham and Sarah, we have welcomed angels in the guise of strangers over the years. When we were not quite one hundred and ninety (more like fifty-eight and fifty-two), the gift of our daughter came to us through our practice of hospitality.

Our adoptive daughter's grandmother was one of our first guests at Manna House, and her biological mother also frequented Manna House. While our daughter's biological mother was in jail, she learned she was pregnant. She asked Kathleen to care for the baby until she got out of jail. Kathleen agreed to do so. The baby was born, and Kathleen brought the newborn home. We were not yet married, but I joined Kathleen in childcare. Kathleen faithfully brought the baby to visit her biological mother. After some nine months, and with her jail sentence extended, the biological mother asked Kathleen to adopt this child.

Kathleen and I talked, prayed, and even laughed from time to time as we discerned our response. We saw the serious responsibility and the humor in what we were being asked to do. As I said, we were not yet married. Kathleen had four older children from a previous marriage, and they would need to welcome this new sibling. I was divorced and without children. Neither Kathleen nor I had plans to get married anytime soon, much less to have a child. God had other plans. A year later, we married and soon adopted our daughter.

Since then, we have reflected many times on the story of Abraham and Sarah as we continue to offer hospitality at Manna House and to our child. Out of that story come these connections between hospitality and parenting.

Love

Love is required to practice hospitality and caregiving. But what is love, and how do we practice love with the stranger in hospitality and the stranger in our child? For Christians, our vision and practice of hospitality are grounded in God's loving hospitality and parenting. God's hospitality begins in God's first act of welcoming love. In Genesis God lovingly creates a world that is good, indeed very good. God, as a loving, hospitable parent, creates a home into which we are welcomed (see Genesis 1–2).

In the exodus story, God liberates Israel from slavery in Egypt, an inhospitable place, and offers Israel hospitality in the desert. Eventually, God welcomes them into a new home, a promised land. Beyond Exodus God continually provides for Israel's needs and instructs them through the Law how to live out their call to be God's people. Through the Law and the Prophets, God holds Israel accountable to practice the hospitality they received, to be a hospitable people who welcome the poor, the widow, and the stranger.[1] God's hospitable care lovingly offers life and liberation to Israel and is illustrated with the image of God as a loving parent: "Can a woman forget her nursing child, or show no compassion for the child of her womb? Even these may forget, yet I will not forget you" (Isaiah 49:15).

In Jesus Christ, God's loving hospitality explicitly extends to all humanity. Mary and Joseph combine hospitality and parenting as they welcome the newborn Jesus under the daunting circumstances of no room at the inn (Luke 2:1-20) and the flight to Egypt (Matthew 2:1-22). Jesus calls us to practice the love received through God's hospitality (John 13:34), to welcome children (Matthew 19:13-14), the stranger (Matthew 25:31-46), and our enemies (Matthew 5:44-45). Hospitality offered in love is an expected practice throughout the New Testament and continues throughout Christian history.[2]

What does this loving practice of hospitality have to do with love in Christian child-rearing? We might first consider how a new child is a stranger to be welcomed. Each child, like every human being, remains a mystery, a person known to God before being known by parents (see Psalm 139:15-16). When we welcome a child as caregivers, we accept a significant disruption of life and an increase in stress. We also take on a financial burden.[3] The social expectation, and hopefully our own expectation, is that with these realities we will welcome the child with love. But biblical love, as practiced in hospitality, may sharpen our practice of parental love. We can see this when we consider the New Testament concept of love as *agape*, self-sacrificial love, in relation to hospitality.

Agape stands in contrast with two other Greek words for love, *eros* and *philia*. Eros is love based on attraction. Philia is the love between friends and social equals. Both of those kinds of love are evident in parenting. Most caregivers would not describe a child as ugly and reprehensible. And who does not hope that, at some point, there might be something approaching friendship with an adult child? However, in welcoming a newborn and for much of parenting, what needs to be practiced, as in hospitality, is agape, which is self-giving, even sacrificial, love.[4] (Some important limits on this self-giving will be discussed later under "Limits.") It is realistic to note that parental love is costly and not always returned by our children. This reality does not discount the joys of caregiving but recognizes that parental love, like love offered in hospitality, is not dependent on reciprocity. In hospitable love, children are not welcomed for what they offer in return but because they are made in the image of God with their own inherent dignity.

As much as we rightfully have expectations for our children's behavior, our expectations should reflect God's love for each child. As the adults in the relationship, we need to temper our expectations in light of our children's own worth and well-being as made in God's image. The practice of loving hospitality applied to parenting rejects the reduction of any child to the desire for the "perfect child." Caregiving shaped by hospitality recognizes human dignity beyond any caregiving expectations or demands. Love in hospitality affirms each person as created in the image of God as children of God. Parental love, like hospitality, involves us in the "harsh and dreadful" realities of love.[5] This is not love in the abstract but in the very concrete realities of parenting, diapers and discipline, temper tantrums and time-outs, and the roller coaster of the big emotions of a child.

This brings me to a crucial ingredient for love in hospitality and caregiving. Our love for others is nourished by God's love for us. Love's demand to offer respect and recognition is only possible through prayer, worship, and times of solitude.[6] Love has an inherent mysticism. Through God's grace, we come to see the stranger as made in the image of God, as the very presence of Christ. To love and welcome the stranger, including our child, we have to be fed by God in prayer and worship. In those holy times with God, we ask that we might see our child as God sees them, as God's child. In prayer we experience God's hospitality through God's unbounded love for us as God's children. Through God's gracious love for us, we come to practice self-giving love (John 13:34-35).

Listening

Listening is a fundamental expression of love as recognition and respect. When the songs of our hearts are not heard and our dreams are not listened to, when our most intimate thoughts are not heard, relationships end.[7] Listening is a fundamental practice for hospitality and caregiving. Being heard is central to how persons are recognized and affirmed with dignity. Listening makes relationships possible. But what does it mean to listen?

At Manna House listening means we welcome guests without rushing through giving things. Rather, we take time to listen to our guests' stories, concerns, and even complaints. To serve our guests well and offer hospitality with respect and recognition, we must listen. Like the practice of love, listening also draws on Christian mysticism. Listening with hospitality requires openness to hearing the voice of God in other persons. Richard Rohr shares how a classic of Christian mysticism, *The Cloud of Unknowing*, asks us first to "enter the Cloud of Forgetting—to forget all our certitudes, all our labels, all our explanations, just forget them!"[8] In this place, we drop "the absolute arrogance of 'knowing' and of being convinced we do know and no one else knows like we know,"[9] and we let go of our hurts and our labels. We may then enter into the Cloud of Unknowing, where we actually do not need to label anymore; that is, we do not need to know that we know. In this Cloud of Unknowing, we stand with the humble openness essential to listening. We become open to listen for a reality that is larger than us, always more than who we are—to listen for our connection with another.

In caregiving, we also need to practice patient and humble listening. We must take time to listen to our children. This requires that we create space in our hearts and homes for listening. The family dinner table is one traditional place for the sharing of stories, news, and points of view. The decline of this practice might lead to a decline in listening. But we should also look for other spaces for listening, such as car rides to and from school, vacations, and shared reading. We always have opportunities to hear our children: during snack time or a visit to an ice cream shop, and in quiet moments before bed. Truly listening to our children offers them the opportunity to share who they are, their experiences, their hopes, desires, and fears. We should draw on the ample advice available for parents to improve our listening.[10]

Within Christian caregiving, our call to listen is inspired and guided by God's listening. God lovingly listens in the exodus story when God hears the cry of the Israelites and listens to their call for freedom (Exodus 3:7-12). God hears the cry of the poor, the oppressed, the excluded, the suffering.[11] In the New Testament, Jesus hears those who the world wants to silence and exclude, such as the woman with the flow of blood (Luke 8:43-48), blind Bartimaeus (Mark 10:46-52), and children (Matthew 18:2-5, 10; 19:13-14). God listens and responds in a way that is loving, redemptive, and restores human dignity. At the same time, numerous biblical texts call us to listen to God, and God speaks in ways we may not expect.[12]

Ed Loring, as a hospitality practitioner, urges going outside of our usual and comfortable places to go to the "listening posts and seeing sites" to enter the world of the stranger and humbly listen.[13] With our children, we also must travel to listening posts and see sites. I confess this is particularly hard when stuck in the models of parenting I inherited from my parents. My daughter started to refuse to go to school. She simply said she did not want to go. For a few weeks, I was able to cajole and pressure her into getting out of the car and walking into her school. But one day, she sat down on the sidewalk and refused to budge. I was more concerned about my own sense of authority and her need for discipline than listening to her. Ultimately, my wife, Kathleen, learned through careful listening that our daughter was being bullied. She did not want to tattle on those doing the bullying, but neither did she want to continue to be bullied. So she did a sit-down strike. This was a hard lesson for me. Caught up in my own world, I had not listened to my daughter. I had not trusted that she had something important to say. I was not ready to listen to her because I was overly focused on my view. In a word, I needed to listen from her perspective, from her "post." I had to travel outside myself with my ear inclined to her perspective.

I am better prepared to listen to my child when I listen with humility. Humility opens me to listen to those seen as having less important things to say. I have to practice respect and recognition through listening with humility. When I listen in this way, I may hear the very heart of the other person, including my child's heart. And in this way, I also come to *learning*, the third practice parenting can draw from hospitality.

Learning

In hospitality and parenting, when we listen carefully with humility, respect, and recognition, learning becomes possible. We come to know the stranger as a human being but also gain wisdom that invites us into a deeper relationship with God and each other. In the biblical practice of hospitality, mutual transformation occurs between host and guest. As we saw in the story of Abraham and Sarah and my own story, the welcome of strangers led to parenthood. When the disciples on the road to Emmaus welcomed the stranger, he turned out to be Christ known in the breaking of the bread (Luke 24:13-35). Biblical hospitality reveals that learning of God opens us to change. The stranger and the child who are loved as made in the image of God become emissaries of God. Loving and listening open us to learning.

Listening with loving humility, respect, and recognition opens us to learn through curiosity, attentiveness, open-mindedness, and intellectual carefulness.[14] In hospitality I have learned from our guests about poverty, racism, imprisonment, mental illness, and addiction. I have learned from their compassion for one another and for me. They have much to teach, and I have much to learn. They are my professors from the school of the streets. When I respectfully listen, I slow down and learn from their lives' stories. In this learning, I avoid overconfidence in my own knowing and become aware of my perspective's limits.[15]

The same applies to learning from our children. First, we recognize that we *can* learn from them. We drop our sense of being all-knowing and open ourselves to the possibility that a child may lead us (Isaiah 11:6). Jesus urged us to "change and become like children" and to welcome a child as if welcoming him (Matthew 18:1-5). Second, we must slow down so we can learn from the child's perspective. I need patience and receptivity when I walk with my daughter because she often stops as dandelions, a bird's eggshell, mud, sticks, and flowers come into her purview. She is learning, but so am I. A child approaches the world with wonder, reverence, and questions. Learning from them is a gift for us.

This learning requires love, respect, and humility. Learning from a person on the streets and from a child teaches us to hold tentatively our beliefs and our ways of doing things. Further, a child's questions and even a child's testing of the necessary discipline and direction we give can feed our humble willingness to learn, revise our perspectives when given good reasons, and critically examine our own views and ways of doing things. Humility clarifies that we may be wrong.

Humility, however, should not be confused with humiliation or accepting wrongdoing. Listening, learning, and loving work together to offer a hospitable space in which we learn from each other. But order is also needed for this to happen, which brings us to the fourth and final hospitality practice that can inform parenting: limits.

Limits

The love we practice in biblical hospitality has limits. Limits are necessary for hospitality in which we love, listen, and learn. God's work of creation provides a hospitable place through limits. God creates an order with light and darkness, water and land, plants and animals; and Scripture's constant refrain is "it was good" (Genesis 1). God's loving hospitality and ours require a just order with limits that neither tolerate nor accept the denigration and harm of others. Parents practice this loving hospitality by setting limits that invite growth into a good life.

Truth-telling, including accountability to a truth beyond us, is a primary limit within hospitality and parenting. We are called, as Ignatius urged, "to put a good interpretation on a neighbor's statement [rather] than to condemn it."[16] Ignatius was not saying that every statement by every person is true. But correction should be undertaken in love to discern what truth may be found even in a mistake. For caregivers, recognizing the relativity of truth certainly means that though we learn from our children, our children are not always right, and our children obviously need to be listeners and learners. Our creative task is to be open to learning from our children and clear with our expectations that seek their growth—intellectually, morally, and spiritually. Our correction considers their stage of life and what tasks they face in growing toward maturity.

A second limit in hospitality and caregiving is justice. Justice seeks the well-being of all through the structuring of the right relationships. Biblical justice requires a shared life that seeks the well-being of all, tested by the standard of how the "least of these" are treated. If the most vulnerable are respected, then we can be sure that all are treated with respect. Hospitality and caregiving justly require discipline that invites growth in respect for others. Literature identifies the need for just limits in the lives of children.[17] Such limits provide a structure for children within which they discover how to live well with others and be just in their relationships.

A third limit in hospitality is boundaries. Boundaries provide the structure within which the practice of hospitality is made possible. To say yes, we sometimes have to say no. We cannot meet every need, nor can we offer hospitality 24/7. To give of self, we must have a self to give, which requires self-care and a recognition of our human limits. Manna House, like all places of hospitality, has limited hours. Our closed hours allow us to prepare the space for hospitality and to take time for our own needs—for rest, relaxation, and renewal. God created the world and rested on the seventh day. We are enjoined to take sabbath as well. Jesus sometimes withdrew from the crowds and went out to quiet places to pray (Matthew 14:13, 23; Mark 1:35, 6:46-47; Luke 4:42, 6:12; John 6:15).

In parenting we need time and space not to respond to our children's needs. We need to practice boundaries in such things as parents' night out, daycare, or quiet time after a child has gone to bed. We need to find a rhythm in parenting in which we are available to our children to love, listen, and learn because we have taken sabbath.

What to Conclude?

The practice of hospitality provides four strategies to assist us in parenting: love, listening, learning, and limits. With those we may offer a hospitable space for our children to be welcomed, treated with respect, heard, and valued for who they are—children of God. Such practices invite us to hopeful and realistic parenting. Our hope comes from God's loving hospitality in our lives. God loves us, listens to our deepest needs, and shows us how to respond with wisdom to those needs. At the same time, God realistically provides limits to wisely structure our lives, remind us of our need for change, and redemptively hold us accountable for our sins. This hope and realism ground our own practice of hospitality. Within hospitality and parenting, we seek life together marked by a love in which we respect and recognize one another as God's children. We listen and learn from the stranger, including the stranger who is our very own child.

Questions for Discussion

1. What does it mean to offer hospitality to children? How might that be different than traditional models of parenting and caregiving?
2. In one section of the chapter, Gathje mentions that love is sustained through such practices as prayer and worship. What spiritual practices help you sustain

love? How might your faith community help families nurture these practices?
3. In this model of hospitality, what role does discipline play?
4. What personal steps would it take to cultivate the practice of listening that Gathje discusses?

Notes

1. See, for example, "When an alien resides with you in your land, you shall not oppress the alien. The alien who resides with you shall be to you as the native-born among you; you shall love the alien as yourself, for you were aliens in the land of Egypt: I am the Lord your God" (Leviticus 19:3-34 and Isaiah's call to hospitality in Isaiah 58:6-9).

2. See Romans 12:13; 1 Corinthians 12–13; Hebrews 13:1-2; 1 Peter 4:9; Revelation 21–22.

3. Many articles detail the challenges and costs of having a child. For example, Andrew Flowers, "Putting a Price Tag on the Stress of Having a Child," ABC News, June 11, 2015, https://fivethirtyeight.com/features/putting-a-price-tag-on-the-stress-of-having-a-child/.

4. There is a long and compelling discussion in Christian ethics regarding this agape love, the love that calls us to self-sacrifice. It is worth noting a debate among those who call for utter disregard for the well-being of oneself with no concern for mutuality or reciprocity in this agape love and those who emphasize that self-sacrifice remains open to a redemptive hope for mutuality in love. In that latter view, Jesus' death on the cross as a symbol and reality of agape love does not lead to his negation but to his resurrection providing a model for this redemptive hope for mutuality, for the creation of a loving community.

5. The language is a nod to Dorothy Day, who often quoted from Dostoyevsky's *Brothers Karamazov*, "Love in action is a harsh and dreadful thing compared to love in dreams." For example, see Michael Boover, *15 Days of Prayer with Dorothy Day* (Hyde Park, NY: New City Press, 2013), 124.

6. Christine D. Pohl, *Making Room: Recovering Hospitality as a Christian Tradition* (Grand Rapids: Eerdmans, 1999), 13.

7. Beyonce, "Listen," lyrics accessed at http://www.songlyrics.com/beyonce-knowles/listen-lyrics/.

8. "Entering the Cloud of Unknowing," Center for Action and Contemplation, March 24, 2023, https://cac.org/daily-meditations/entering-the-cloud-of-unknowing-2023-03-24/. Adapted from Richard Rohr, *Beginner's Mind* (Albuquerque: Center for Action and Contemplation, 2002).

9. "Entering the Cloud of Unknowing."

10. E.g., https://centerforparentingeducation.org/library-of-articles/healthy-communication/the-skill-of-listening/ and https://www.cdc.gov/parenting-toddlers/about/index.html?CDC_AAref_Val=https://www.cdc.gov/parents/essentials/toddlersandpreschoolers/communication/activelistening.html%2520%2520.

11. See, e.g., Exodus 22:23; Job 34:28; Psalm 6:8, 10:17, 18:6, 40:1, 55:17, 69:33, 116:2, 145:18-19; Proverbs 21:13; Isaiah 65:24; Jeremiah 33:3.

12. See 1 Kings 19:11-13; Job 37:14; Psalm 46:10, 102:17, 116:2; Proverbs 8:32; Isaiah 28:9, 23, 33, 55:2-3; Jeremiah 22:29; Matthew 11:15; 1 John 4:6.

13. Ed Loring, "Death-Row Visitation: A Listening Post and a Seeing Site," in *A Work of Hospitality: The Open Door Reader 1982-2002*, ed. Peter R. Gathje (Atlanta: The Open Door Community, 2002): 190–93.

14. Jason Baehr, "Intellectual Virtues, Civility, and Public Discourse," in Evan Rosa and Gregg Ten Elshof, eds., *Virtue and Voice: Habits of Mind for a Return to Civil Discourse* (Abilene, TX: Abilene Christian University Press, 2019), 6.

15. Baehr, 33–36.

16. See Sam Sawyer, "The Poison of Polarization and the Catholic Call to Communion," *America* Magazine, April 2023, 24.

17. For example, https://evolvetreatment.com/blog/setting-boundaries-kids/ and https://www.canr.msu.edu/news/boundaries_and_expectations_are_important_parenting_tools.

"But Why?"

EMILY A. PECK

When my first child was a toddler, they entered the "why" stage. I knew it was coming. It is traditional toddler folklore, almost given as a warning: "Just wait until they start asking why!" It is an interesting part of the parenting journey. I decided to think of this as a game. This has served me well with each of my three kids, actually. I try to answer each "But why?" until the toddler becomes tired of asking the question. Believe me, it can take a while—a long while. But also, answering their questions can help you stay entertained for a long car trip.

I realized that what I was doing through this game was helping my children know they can approach this world with all their questions. They do not have to take things at face value. They can and should ask why. This is exciting! This is empowering! They have brains to use!

I realized quickly, too, as I began this game, that there would be times when I could not answer the why. Sometimes it's because of that frustrating toddler circular logic:

> Toddler: Can I have my socks?
> Me: Yes.
> Toddler: Why?

Me: Because you asked for them.
Toddler: But why?
Me: . . .

Other times the frustration is because I have no idea how to answer the why, because even for a toddler, there are some questions I cannot answer. And I am a theological school professor and ordained minister. Some are the big questions of life and death. "But why did my friend's home catch on fire?" Sometimes, although I think I know the answer based on my education, I have no idea how to explain it to a toddler. "But why do people vote for someone who will not treat them well?" I also realized the game was much more fun when I knew the answers. One thing seems true about parenting: parents might be made when they have a child, but they develop along with their kids. When I could not finish the game—when one of my kids asked why and I could not answer—it put me in the humble position of admitting what my kids will certainly know as they become teenagers: I do not know everything. These little beings depend on me for everything, but they already have questions I cannot answer, which are humbling and terrifying but also exactly right.

I have learned from parenting through the why stage (which, let's be honest, is really for all of childhood) that being human is being limited. I might know some things about some things and maybe even many things about some things. But knowing something about everything or many things about everything is not going to happen, especially when it comes to God. I have long known that God is too big (or too other, too transcendent, or too, perhaps, *godly*) to fit in my head. My confirmation students love to prove this when they ask, "Can God make a rock so big that God can't move it?" Knowing that I do not know all the answers—especially when it comes to God—as a parent is challenging, exhilarating, and scary.

Lois Lowry's novel *Gossamer* is one of my favorites. The book has two sets of characters. One set contains a young child who is in foster care, his foster mother, and his biological mother, who is working on piecing her life back together so she can regain custody of him. The other set are dream-givers who collect stories and memories around people's homes, bestowing dreams on them. The dream-givers intentionally educate the newest member of their group, teaching how to collect fragments of memories, bestow dreams, and what to do if a nightmare comes. At the beginning of the book, the newest dream-giver, Littlest, is paired with an older dream-giver named Fastidious. Littlest asks lots of questions. She is like the toddler always asking why. Her questions of Fastidious, though, concern her desire to know what she is. She asks so many questions that Fastidious becomes annoyed, saying, "Stop that questioning! You insisted on coming. You said you'd be quiet. My nerves are becoming frayed. I want no more questions now. None whatsoever."[1] Littlest promises to stop asking questions, but a page later, she has forgotten her promise and asks, "Might we be *human*?"[2] Soon thereafter, Littlest receives a new mentor, Thin Elderly, who has more of a sense of humor and responds to her many questions with welcome. They learn from each other as the book continues.

I love the pair of Thin Elderly and Littlest because his welcoming of her questions allows her imagination to flourish and for her to do things he has never thought of before. It enables him to learn from her, something he seems not to have expected. I often think about this pair as a wonderful analogy for faith formation. When we are parenting and caregiving and trying to raise faithful children, how might we be more like Thin Elderly and less like Fastidious?

The Power of Wondering

Godly Play, a Montessori-based Christian education curriculum in which the Bible storyteller makes wondering statements to encourage open responses from children, is a method some Christian educators embrace for welcoming questions. Wondering questions are encouraged in different settings, including one-on-one conversations with children,[3] churches that are trying to do a new thing,[4] and in reading Bible stories at home.[5]

Jerome Berryman, *Godly Play*'s creator, says, "Wondering opens the creative process and draws both the lesson and the child's life experiences into the person's creation of meaning."[6] Berryman juxtaposes with the Socratic method of education. He says, "The general difference between a Socratic strategic question and a *Godly Play* wondering is that the teacher knows where the Socratic questions are leading while wondering does not."[7] As Berryman explains, wondering allows children to acknowledge and explore the "existential limits" that he says "press in on us."[8] These limits are "death, threat of freedom, the need for meaning, and our fundamental aloneness."[9] These topics are difficult to discuss. Each of them might be enough to cause a lump in our throat, for our eyes to widen, for us to want to shut this book and escape, or to call our therapist to schedule an appointment we have been putting off.

Adults are used to confronting and dealing with these limits, even if dealing with them sometimes means turning away or ignoring them. We might not commonly think about our children dealing with these same limits. But they do.

Nothing may be clearer to me as a parent than my limits. I reached my physical limits when caring for children while recovering from C-section surgery, nursing a newborn, and being utterly exhausted and sleep-deprived at the same time. I reached my emotional limits seeing my children struggle with things I have never had to navigate and am not sure how to support them. I did not grow up during a time with social media and electronics addiction, for example. I'm figuring out parenting amid these realities as I go, along with nearly every other parent or caregiver of children now in the early part of the twenty-first century. What we learn will hopefully become good models for the parents who come after us. But they will also have their own challenges in the future, about which I will know nothing. For parents and caregivers who want to raise their children with faith as an important part of their identity and practice, becoming comfortable with our limits around our knowledge of God might be an especially important and difficult piece of the picture.

Part of the challenge, though, is the anxiety it can bring up for us adults as we companion children.

Fear and Anxiety

A gift of the wonderings is that the person who is asking the question cannot possibly know the answer. In *Godly Play*, the storyteller poses the wonderings. Berryman writes, "It is, perhaps, most important to be sure the storyteller joins the children in authentic wondering. If you think you already know the 'answer' to a wondering question, you are not *wondering*!"[10] Part of the challenge with welcoming the questions in homes with children is that adults are sometimes really bad at wondering.

In our careers, adults are supposed to know the answers to questions we are asked. We are fully aware that when our children ask us a question, they are doing so to hear an answer. Children look up to adults, especially the ones responsible for their well-being, and need us to be ready for the uncertainties, inconsistencies, and difficulties life throws at us. Children depend on us, which is a lot of pressure for adults, especially when we struggle also with uncertainties, inconsistencies, and difficulties. Our knee-jerk reaction is telling our kids everything will be okay and affirming we have it under control. The problem is that it might not be and we do not.

In our recent collective history, we experienced a pandemic when we did not know if (or when) everything would be okay. There was a long period of time when we did not have it under control. Of course, not only a pandemic shows this reality. Parenting and caregiving during times of war, drought, famine, school/grocery store/movie theater/church shootings, and political upheaval are other situations that bring collective and communal places of not knowing it will be okay and not having it under control. And then there are individual places of not knowing it will be okay and not having it under control: employment loss, loss of a loved one, loss of one's home, needing to change schools or daycare, divorce, or not knowing where the next meal will come from. There are also the ongoing cultural practices, positions, and sins that cause fear and anxiety for certain groups of people: racially minoritized folks, women, transpeople, and other groups who are oppressed and threatened for their very existence. Still, no matter the situation we are living through, children will look to adults to be stable and responsible. No matter what is going on in our political or personal lives, children will look to adults for the care they need and deserve. Parents and caregivers feel this pressure constantly. When we welcome questions—the whys and the wonderings—I wonder if we might also be welcoming our own limitations, fears, and anxiety.

Parenting and Caregiving in an Anxious Place

Not all anxiety is bad. Not all fear is misplaced. These emotions keep us safe. They help us to maneuver through our days safely by measuring risks, code-switching, and other strategies. Parents and caregivers intentionally teach some of these strategies, while others are taught more implicitly. When a child poses a why or a wondering to a caring adult, even if we want to keep it more implicit, the child brings it out into the light and asks us to address it with them. They trust us, or they would not ask.

In wonderings, the adults ask the questions, and the children answer. Adults do not evaluate the answers or tell the children whether they are right or wrong. How could they? The wonderings, after all, do not have answers. "I wonder what part of the story is the most important" does not have an answer, but it does invite a response from the children.[11] When a toddler leads us down a stream of whys, even if we know some answers or can search the internet for some, a why we cannot answer will come. We will only get to that place, though, if we keep the space and relationship open for the child to continue to ask. We dislike not knowing the answer, and when we reach that point, we are teaching the child that we are only human. What a difficult lesson for both sides of the question—the child who asks and the parent or caregiver who is asked.

Parents and caregivers are challenged to acknowledge when we have reached the limits of our knowledge with our children. Two things happen: (1) we fear we are not providing the child with what they need, and (2) we are afraid we do not know enough. We worry we are inadequate to the parenting task. Like Fastidious in *Gossamer*, we can shut down the questions. We might not even think about why we make this choice, but we make it. It might be almost involuntary. "Stop asking so many questions!" "Okay, that's enough questions for today. Let's get lunch." We might teach implicitly that questions are bad or that too many questions are bad (and how many is too many?). We also might teach implicitly that our kids cannot bring their questions to us or that questions are dangerous. We do not want to teach any of this.

We want to teach that questions are wonderful. We want to teach that the biggest questions a child has are really good ones to ask. We want to teach our children that they can grow emotionally and spiritually through their questions. We want them to learn that doubt is not the antithesis of faith but rather an integral part of it. The problem is that we adults may never have learned this.

But why?

Many adults were never encouraged to question as children. Many were taught by a Socratic method in our Sunday school classrooms. Many of us were raised to be "seen and not heard." Many were taught explicitly that doubt is not only antithetical to faith but actively threatens it. Many were taught that there is always one right answer to a question. All of this might be swirling around in us, along with the two fears mentioned above.

One way to parent in this place of fear and anxiety, a way to learn to welcome the whys and wonderings is to get comfortable asking our own questions. Adult religious education classes and groups can experiment with questioning and wondering. Have a Bible study where no one is allowed to answer any questions, but everyone is invited to ask them. Read Scripture on your own or in groups, and instead of looking for answers, see what wonderings the stories might stir up. Invite parents and caregivers in your faith community to follow journal prompts to guide them to ask the big answerless questions. Support one another when you realize how scary it is to ask questions and how disconcerting it is when there is no answer. When we come to the limits of our knowledge, we reach the beginning of the mystery of God. No matter how much we learn or study, we will never know all there is to know about God.

Acknowledging our humanity and God's divinity has a certain beauty. There is beauty when a community comes together to support one another through the anxiety that differences sometimes create. When adults become more comfortable with this discomfort, we support our children when they reach the limits of their knowledge and their grown-ups' knowledge. Together with children, we can relish the mystery of God and even relish the limits of our humanity. Thanks be to God that there is something bigger than us.

Questions for Discussion

1. What does it look like to implement "wondering" in our relationships with children?
2. How can we acknowledge our fear and anxiety while continuing to be present for children?

3. How can we normalize not knowing in congregational life?

4. Peck notes that children don't need the answers as much as they need the space to hear the questions. How might this sentence help you change the way you might "faith" children? When and how can you ask "wondering questions" with children rather than worrying about the right answers?

5. What images come to mind when you see the words *Godly Play*? What about the why question makes parents uncomfortable?

Notes

1. Lois Lowry, *Gossamer* (New York: Walter Lorraine, 2006), 5.
2. Lowry, *Gossamer*, 6.
3. Tanya Marie Eustace Campen, *Holy Work with Children: Making Meaning Together* (Eugene, OR: Pickwick, 2021), 1.
4. Tim Shapiro, *How Your Congregation Learns: The Learning Journey from Challenge to Achievement* (New York: Rowan & Littlefield, 2017), 86–87.
5. Elizabeth F. Caldwell, *I Wonder: Engaging a Child's Curiosity about the Bible* (Nashville: Abingdon, 2016).
6. Jerome Berryman, *Teaching Godly Play: How to Mentor the Spiritual Development of Children* (Denver: Morehouse Education Resources, 2009), 45.
7. Berryman, *Teaching Godly Play*, 53.
8. Berryman, *Teaching Godly Play*, 67.
9. Berryman, *Teaching Godly Play*, 67.
10. Berryman, *Teaching Godly Play*, 53.
11. Berryman, *Teaching Godly Play*, 49.

Section 1

Good Roots: Caregiver Practices to Build a Foundation of Faith

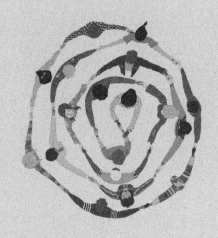

1

"Let the Children Come": One Church's Story of Congregational Transformation

MARY YOUNG

> People were bringing little children to Jesus for him to place his hands on them, but the disciples rebuked them. When Jesus saw this, he was indignant. He said to them, "Let the little children come to me, and do not hinder them, for the kingdom of God belongs to such as these."
> —Mark 10:13-14 (NIV)

Why do so-called well-meaning church folk seem not to have patience for children in their midst? What is it that annoys some adults about children being in the worshiping community? These may be age-old questions for which, in some cases, no satisfactory answers exist. The disciples' actions in the epigraph above speak to a fundamental philosophy about children and the worshiping community. They felt that the children would be a bother to Jesus, so parents should not have brought them to the gathering. Did Jesus have time for children? Well, there is a clear and poignant answer to that question. Jesus was annoyed by how the disciples spoke to the parents. He cautioned against stopping the children and even highlighted their manner and character as illustrative of the kingdom of heaven.

Jesus' words serve as a guide regarding our practices of welcoming children into the worshiping community. Whatever our preconceived notions about their value, worth, and understanding of faith, Jesus lifted them as role models for those seeking to enter the kingdom. What we think about the faith and spirituality of children influences how we embrace them as members of the gathered community. Human development theorists and Christian educators remind us that children also have faith. Sofia Cavalletti asserts that "children have a profound sense of God. This is not only on an intellectual level, but one that is deeply existential. They feel not only awe but love and security."[1] When considering the growth and development of small children, we know that they are drawn to rhymes, songs, and stories. Those seeking to develop faith in children can incorporate these pedagogical practices into religious music, Bible learning, and prayers.

Beyond this, the impact of a spiritual family cannot be overemphasized. Spirituality theologian Peter Feldmeier stresses that "deeply prayerful and spiritually centered parents have a profound effect, albeit an unconscious one, on their young children."[2] This chapter now turns to the role of parenting. In particular this chapter tells how one congregation became surrogate parents for the children God entrusted to their care. As such, not only did the welcoming practices of the church become illustrations of Jesus' mandate to let the children come, but the presence of the children became a catalyst for breathing new life into the congregation.

A Contextual Reality

I once pastored a church in the heart of an urban community, where it had been for ninety-eight years. During its impressive heyday prior to my coming, worshipers needed to arrive almost an hour early to get a good seat. During those years, all age groups were present in the vibrant worshiping faith community. Children participated in various faith formation activities and sang in the children's choir. The church had an active choir for teens, many of whom idolized their pastor and would often follow him and his wife home after worship services. However, by its ninety-eighth year when I arrived, this church had become a very different congregation. The membership had decreased significantly. There were families with children who had grown up in the church throughout the years, but they moved on and out, leaving noticeable gaps in the life-cycle groups for the church. While a remnant of committed leaders and members remained, the church needed a new vision and a fresh beginning that could not only speak to the current congregational needs but also help to lift the members to a place of hope and expectation beyond those relished in former years. What we did not know was that God would use children from our community as the catalysts for breathing new life into the church.

And the Children Came

Couched in a challenging urban context where crime, poverty, and other social concerns abounded, our church needed a good shot in the arm. Like many urban churches, we were on a spot of ground surrounded by both gentrification and urban blight. This dual reality created a challenging context for a small, struggling congregation. As the congregation began to go outside of its walls for ministry and expand its evangelistic footprint, God began to send unexpected blessings. By its ninety-ninth year, through the evangelistic efforts of our young adults, God blessed us with an influx of children from our community. Our church van provided transportation for children who lived in a nearby housing project. When asked if their children could attend worship and other activities at our church, the parents in the housing project were all too happy to release their little ones to our care. In reality the children's coming temporarily released them from the danger of their environment, where they heard gunshots, saw fights, experienced neglect, and went hungry regularly.

The children became evangelists as they told their friends about their experiences at our church, and others wanted to come. The children easily filled three to four pews in the congregation, and their ages ranged from about five to twelve years old. The presence of the children brought new vitality into the congregation and challenged us to develop intentional, relevant, and creative discipleship ministries for them and their families.

Our Church Responded

As a congregation, we were stretched to intentionally include children in the learning and worshiping community. We did not ignore the economic and sociological realities from which they came. They were Black children and youth who were already struggling against some odds. Anne Streaty Wimberly, a longtime youth advocate and mentor, asserts, "Black youth are unique in their disproportionate representation among the poor and jobless, among school dropouts, in single-parent households, in foster care, and in youth detention facilities."[3] Ironically, Wimberly also cites research indicating that these same youth show distinctive patterns in terms of religion. Religious faith and activity are highest among Black youth as a racial group, and they are more likely to pray daily than other groups. More Black protestant youth identify as born-again Christians than other racial groups.[4]

We knew our church's role would be as surrogate and partner in a spiritual parenting process for the children's faith formation. Ironically, though many had never attended church regularly, they had an almost insatiable desire to learn, grow, and be involved. And their coming sparked new energy in our leaders to care for them, guide them, love them, teach them, and ensure that they felt welcomed at our church. The children loved hugs, smiles, and affirmative words, and as their pastor, I gave those things generously each Sunday when they ran to me after the benediction. They were not even aware of their ministry to me! Their unconditional love flowed like fresh dew on a sometimes weary spirit and gave me the energy to anticipate the next great thing God was up to with our congregation. The congregational ministry with the children included actions that met both their spiritual and physical needs. We became revitalized in wonderful ways.

Church School Expansion

Almost immediately, we went from having no children's Sunday school class to having a bustling group of learners who required two teachers for different age groups. Our driver could not transport all of them in the van with one trip, which resulted in at least two trips each Sunday. Downstairs, where the classes were held, our teachers were busy organizing the day's lesson, but just as important, they were preparing a nutritious breakfast for the little ones who would come in hungry. After all, we were the hands and feet of Christ they would experience that morning. While in our care, they were fed both physical and spiritual food. After the children's classes were dismissed, they came upstairs to the main sanctuary and had an opportunity to share highlights from their classes. Our teachers sharpened their skills at organizing the children and were inspired and energized by the children's excitement to learn and participate.

Organization of Weekly Tutorial and Bible Study Sessions for Children

Sunday worship and study opportunities mushroomed into a midweek tutorial program and Bible study session. Our church's many active and retired educators now had a great call to use their gifts with the children. Leaders eagerly volunteered to teach math, reading, writing, and other subjects. A designated amount of time was spent in tutoring and the remaining time in a brief age-appropriate Bible study. As on Sundays, Wednesday night also included snacks for the children. Our young adults were major drivers for this work and creatively used other talents and gifts in the church to keep the program sustained and working well. For instance, some members were asked to prepare snacks for the children, while others provided tutoring. Still others agreed to be on hand for questions or concerns and to clean the space after the evening's activities. Members of the clergy team were sometimes called on to do the brief Bible study. Through the ministry with the children, church members knew they were making an impact on these young lives, and they embraced the reciprocal life-giving energy that emanated from the children.

Involvement of Children in the New Member Orientation Program

The church began to see a spiritual hunger for church membership among the older children. They became curious about baptism and Communion. This created another point of connection with the parents and caregivers of the children. Ministry team members would contact the children's caretakers and indicate their desire to become members of our congregation. They also invited parents to orientation sessions.

Leaders of our new member orientation program saw the benefit of having youth representation on the committee and thus involved older youth who had already been baptized in the sessions where older children were preparing for baptism. This inspired leadership among the youth and added a welcomed perspective to the otherwise adult-only committee. Young baptismal candidates glowed when they saw someone closer to their own age in the room. Our adult leaders focused on ways to have the young leader share their experience in joining the church. Additionally, our leaders were stretched to keep what they would share simple enough for a child to understand. A successful orientation process involved attendance at two to three sessions, parental accompaniment at the sessions, and selection of a date for baptism. If not at the orientation sessions, parents always showed up for the actual baptism. In some instances, this was the one event that brought a parent to the church. We saw several children lead their parents to faith.

Sponsoring a Summer Enrichment Camp

As the school year ended and summer vacation began, our church wanted to offer enrichment activities for the neighborhood's scores of children. Many of them would not be participating in any camps or Christian learning experiences unless neighboring churches held free events. We offered a one-week half-day program that included meals, activities, a field trip, games, and learning. This meant "all hands on deck" for the congregation. Church members rallied around this program and volunteered their time, talents, and treasure to make it happen. The sheer joy of contributing to this program kept many members engaged during the entire week. Some came to the church just to be around in case of any needs. Others gathered donations of snacks, supplies, and other items from local businesses to help offset the program's cost. Members took great pride in actively contributing to the camp's success. We began to see the incredible energy, fellowship, and engagement that working together brought among our adult leaders as they invested in this project. Our church was being blessed in ways we had not even imagined.

Children and Youth Worship Leadership and Participation

We recognized that the children needed more involvement in the Sunday morning worship experience. Figuring out a more hands-on approach provided an opportunity for the congregation to mentor these young leaders through worship. This mentoring, known as observational learning, is an important faith formation process in worship.[5]

Our church designated one Sunday a month for youth worship leading. We mentored young people to serve as worship leaders, while others led in additional aspects of the order of worship. Our young adults spent time preparing these young leaders for the roles in which they would serve. Through these experiences, the children learned simple prayers and public speaking skills. They were also called on to exhibit ambition, bravery, teamwork, and responsibility. Our congregation learned through this process that parents, caregivers, and spiritual leaders of children must take the time and exercise patience to let children lead the way. By giving children opportunities to lead in worship, the congregation can encourage children when they make mistakes, affirm them amid their doubts, and be open to the ways God will use them to inspire our own faith.

Adoption of a Community School

We learned that several children connected to our church attended a neighborhood elementary school with many needs. The resources at the school were scarce, and the school needed volunteers to read to students and assist with other matters. Our church decided to adopt this school and support the teachers and leaders who worked so hard for children in our community. A small leadership team from our church and I had a meeting with the principal to ascertain in what ways we might be helpful. Our visit provided good information on how to move forward.

The church agreed to buy school supplies; provide the children with hats, gloves, and coats for the winter months; assist with tutoring needs; and visit classes to read to the younger children. As the pastor, I found my times at the school especially gratifying as children from the church would see me and run excitedly to greet me in the hallway. Our church knew the children needed to see our faces and be assured that we cared about every aspect of their lives. The church kids proudly boasted to their school friends when they saw someone from our church at their school.

As with the summer program, this ministry venture yielded an overflow of participation and contributions. We distributed a list of items to our members that they could provide and asked them to deposit them in a box in the narthex of our church. The congregation gave so much that we had to provide two large boxes for the collections. This giving opportunity energized our congregation and allowed us to demonstrate love in action. Our church members began to desire more ministry opportunities beyond the church's four walls. More importantly, their theological worldviews about ministry broadened and enlarged.

Conclusion: This Is What We Learned

Through these and other impromptu experiences, our church was inspired toward new life and ministry as we celebrated the children in our midst. We learned as much from the children as they learned from us. We treasured these epiphanies in our work with the children:

- The children showed us how to work together as a congregation.
- Ministry to the children brought out the best in our services of time, talent, and treasure.
- Our work stretched us to be welcoming and affirming of children in our midst.
- Our ministry of Christian education was expanded as we focused on creative faith formation activities designed specifically for children.
- We learned that when we pray for change, we must be ready for how God will bring it about.

Believing that intentional religious activity is important for early childhood spiritual formation, our congregation fully embraced this gift of children. We were convinced that our children would have faith in the future. We wanted both the preschool and elementary-age children in our church to imagine and experience God through the community of our congregation. Human development theorist John Westerhoff believes that such initial encounters, grounded in the child's vivid and developing imagination, are foundational for further faith development.[6] It was no wonder to us that Jesus said, "Let the little children come to me, and do not hinder them, for the kingdom of heaven belongs to such as these" (Matthew 19:14, NIV). Their innocence and love for the ways of Christ refreshed our comfortable and complacent faith community. We welcomed the children as affirmation and confirmation of God's vision for developing our congregation, particularly as it related to our role in an urban neighborhood. We now had someone to pass our faith stories to and to ensure that future generations would know the meaning of our stones (Joshua 4:21).

Questions for Discussion

1. Are there children in your geographical community? How are children involved in your faith community? How might they be involved?
2. What challenges do you face in involving children in the life of the faith community?

Notes

1. Sofia Cavalletti, *The Religious Potential of the Child*, trans. Patricia and Julie Coulter (Chicago: Liturgy Training Publications, 1992), 35.
2. Peter Feldmeier, *The Developing Christian: Spiritual Growth Through the Life Cycle* (New York: Paulist Press, 2007), 93.
3. Anne Streaty Wimberly, ed. *Keep It Real: Working with Today's Black Youth* (Nashville: Abingdon, 2005), xiii.
4. Wimberly, *Keep It Real*, xiii.
5. Albert Bandura (1901–94) was a psychologist who developed social learning theory. He studied children to understand how they learn from others. His studies showed that children imitate one another because they observe and copy others' actions. The process has come to be known as observational learning.
6. John Westerhoff, *Will Our Children Have Faith?* (Toronto: Anglican Book Centre, 2000), 89ff.

2

Children's Bibles and Your Child

RUSSELL W. DALTON

Children's Bibles are among the most common religious education publications sold in the United States. They help to establish children's understanding of what the Bible is and the nature of faith. The choices we make regarding which children's Bibles to purchase and read to our children are vital to our efforts in raising faithful children.

Upon our third child's birth, my wife and I received a children's Bible from a fellow church member. The title proclaimed it was a children's Bible for little girls. It had a pink cover and contained charming, cartoonish illustrations of biblical women who were often shown holding a broom or baking. For example, the story of "Mrs. Noah" was titled "Whatever You Say, Dear." It showed "Mrs. Noah" cooking and cleaning. She was not happy about having to share the ark with all those "smelly animals," especially the spiders. Still, she told Noah, "Whatever you say, dear." The children's Bible concluded each story with a lesson on "Becoming a Woman of God." For the story of Mrs. Noah, the lesson was "A Woman of God Is Obedient," and it was clear from the context that this meant obeying her husband as well as obeying God.[1]

My wife and I chose not to read that children's Bible to our children. While some may agree with this children's

Bible author and illustrator's view on traditional gender roles promoted in the book, we did not. Furthermore, we felt the cartoonish illustrations potentially trivialized the stories of the Bible. Also, the Bible characters were depicted as white people with rosy cheeks. We did not want our children to grow up viewing the Bible in a way they might dismiss as a book of cartoons or fairy tales when they grew up, nor did we want them thinking the Middle Eastern people of the Bible were white. Finally, this children's Bible took great liberties in recreating and retelling Bible stories to help make a particular point. Far from teaching our children basic biblical literacy, this book would miseducate our children about the Bible's stories. Those lessons, if learned in our children's formative years, would be hard to unlearn later in life.

Our church friend who generously gave us this children's Bible would likely have shared our concerns. She probably simply saw a colorful, fun-looking Bible. Like many parents and caregivers who buy children's Bibles, she may have made just a simple assessment before making her purchase.

Evaluating the Changes Children's Bibles Make to Bible Stories

As was the case with the book described above, most children's Bibles do not simply retell Bible stories objectively and neutrally. The gift of that children's Bible inspired me to undertake a long journey of researching and reading hundreds of children's Bibles, examining how children's Bible authors and illustrators consciously or unconsciously revise Bible stories in ways that promote their own views on theology and morality.[2] By being aware of these adaptations, we can better evaluate which children's Bibles may be best for our children.

I recommend that, as much as possible, adults include their children in the process of evaluating and choosing a children's Bible or, alternatively, choosing not to read a children's Bible at all. Even if children do not have an adult understanding of the issues involved in this choice, they have valuable perspectives to offer, and they will appreciate being granted some agency in their religious education. Furthermore, by talking through these issues with your child, the process of choosing a children's Bible (or not) will provide children with a valuable lesson in biblical literacy.

Children's Bible authors and illustrators adapt and change Bible stories in at least four ways. Adults and children will want to consider each of these as they evaluate various children's Bibles.

Embellishments and Additions

Children's Bibles often add scenes and details to Bible stories not in the canonical text. Some embellishments have been around for centuries. Still, children's Bible authors seem to use these embellishments or create their own scenes to serve certain theological or moral agendas.

For example, some children's Bible authors have added various scenes to the story of Noah's ark. Some, for the purpose of teaching children to fear an all-powerful God's judgment, describe children and adults climbing to mountaintops to escape the floodwaters and screaming to be allowed in the ark. Others, before suggesting that children today should repent and turn to God before it is too late, add scenes of Noah's neighbors mocking Noah while he warns them the flood is coming. Still others have added detailed descriptions of how Noah worked hard and never complained to teach children that they should do the same. The book of Genesis contains no such scenes, but some children's Bible authors add them to serve their own educational agendas.[3]

With this in mind, adults and children need to assess what a children's Bible has added to Bible stories, why the authors might make those additions, and whether they are comfortable with those changes.

Erasures

Another way that children's Bibles change Bible stories can be found in what they leave out. Sometimes this seems to be to simplify the story. For example, God commands Noah to gather seven pairs of clean animals and one pair each of unclean animals to take on the ark (Genesis 7:2-3). This story is almost always abridged to say that Noah simply gathered one pair of every animal. Sometimes children's Bibles leave out stories that are deemed inappropriate for young readers. For example, the awkward story of Noah becoming drunk and falling asleep naked after the flood is rarely mentioned in children's Bibles of the past century.

In recent years, a growing number of children's Bibles make no mention that anyone died in the flood or even that God was the one who caused the flood, especially in children's Bibles intended for younger children. God merely warns Noah that the flood is coming to keep him and his family safe.[4] The story is retold and illustrated as a fun boat ride with animal friends.[5] This version of the story may be more age-appropriate for young children, but parents and caregivers might ask themselves whether the story of a fun boat ride with animals is still the biblical story of Noah's ark.

When evaluating children's Bibles, therefore, it is helpful to ask, "What is being left out, and are the deletions incidental or significant to the Bible story?"

Illustrations

Many adults' most vivid memories of the children's Bibles from their childhood are the illustrations included with the stories. Bible scholar David Gunn suggests that these illustrations likely carry more lasting interpretive power than the texts of children's Bibles.[6]

In reviewing a children's Bible's illustrations, we can ask ourselves several important questions. What impression do the illustrations give about the nature of the Bible? Are the illustrations realistic, depicting the scenes as historical events or important ancient stories? Or are the illustrations more cartoonish like other modern children's picture books? For example, many recent children's Bible versions of the story of Noah's ark depict the animals on the ark acting in unrealistic ways, such as folding their hands while kneeling in prayer, hanging up laundry, dancing on two feet, or playing marbles with Noah.[7] Illustrations of anthropomorphic animal friends for Noah may be fun and entertaining, but they risk trivializing the story for children and treating it as a fairy tale rather than as a sacred text.

Another important consideration is how the illustrations depict Bible characters. For much of American history, most children's Bibles have been written, illustrated, and published by white people and have depicted the people of the Bible as white people of Western European descent. These illustrations give children the erroneous impression that the people of the Bible were white rather than Middle Eastern people of color with a variety of skin tones. Fortunately, in the twenty-first century, a growing number of children's Bibles are illustrating Bible characters with various skin tones and facial features.[8] These illustrations carry significant educational value for both children of color and for white children.

Adding Theological and Moral Commentary

Very few biblical narratives end by giving readers a specific theological lesson to be learned or a moral to the story. Instead, the stories are told, and readers are left to reflect on them and draw their own insights. Many religious educators see this as a strength of biblical literature. Children are particularly good at responding to stories and making applications to their own lives.

Unfortunately, many children's Bibles try to "fix" this open-ended nature of the Bible by telling their readers the one theological or moral lesson they should find in each story. Often when reading these children's Bibles, it is difficult to tell when the retelling of the actual Bible story ends and when the author's sermonizing begins. Some of the best religious education we can provide children is to read them stories and to wonder together about the stories' meanings and implications for our lives rather than having children's Bible authors provide us with their interpretations.

When evaluating children's Bibles, children and adults can ask themselves whether they agree with the interpretations and applications the children's Bible provides for a particular story. What other interpretations or lessons might be learned from that story? Would it be better for the children's Bible simply to retell the stories and leave them open for interpretation?

Choosing a Bible or a Children's Bible

Given these issues with children's Bibles mentioned above, what options do parents, caregivers, religious educators, and children have when choosing a Bible or children's Bible? People have taken at least four different approaches to answering that question.

Do Not Have Children Read the Bible

The first approach some adults take is simply to withhold the Bible from children until they are older. This is not necessarily common, but it is an approach many people have taken over the years. Some suggest that the Bible is too complex for children, and therefore reading the Bible to children would only serve to confuse them about religion. Others are concerned that the Bible's stories of sex, violence, and horror make it inappropriate for children. As religious educator Ronald Goldman wrote, "[The Bible] is written by adults for adults and is plainly not a children's book."[9] Instead of taking liberties with the biblical text to turn it into a child-friendly storybook, parents and guardians who take this approach choose to wait until children are older before introducing them to Bible reading. Instead, they might find other quality children's books to read to their children that might instill good moral and spiritual values.[10]

Have Children Read the Bible Itself

A second approach some choose is for children to read or be read full translations of the Bible. Some may prefer this approach because it gives children unfiltered access to the biblical text.

Adults can read a respected translation of the Bible, such as the New Revised Standard Version Updated Edition, along with children. They can then discuss problematic and confusing words, provide helpful cultural background, and wonder along with children about what the passage may have to say to us today.

When I was growing up, my family regularly had family devotions. We read from a full translation of the Bible, and all five of us children were allowed to ask questions and offer perspectives on the Bible. Our parents never shamed us for asking any questions or offering unusual interpretations. As a result, we each grew up confident in our ability to read the Bible thoughtfully, and we continued to do so as adults.

Today some translations are available that are more directly accessible to young children. For example, the New Century Version (NCV) translates the Hebrew and Greek from the original text into third-grade reading level English. The New International Reader's Version (NIrV), based on the New International Version, is an evangelical translation that also attempts to translate the original text to a third-grade reading level.

Choose a Children's Bible That Attempts to Stay Close to the Biblical Text

Those whose goal is for their children to gain biblical literacy might choose to avoid children's Bibles that significantly change Bible stories. They may, however, still want children to have access to a children's Bible that selects key stories, leaves out content deemed inappropriate for children, includes engaging illustrations, and tells the stories of the Bible in language that is easy for them to understand.[11]

Those who take this approach will want to review several children's Bibles, comparing how they retell the stories to the way the stories appear in the Bible. They can then choose one that, in their assessment, adheres closely to the words and events as they appear in the Bible and includes more realistic illustrations of Bible characters as people of Middle Eastern descent.[12]

In recalling the simple childish tales that they once read in children's Bibles, some have grown up and dismissed the Bible as a book of fairy tales for children. Because of these concerns, some may wish to avoid children's Bibles that illustrate Bible stories in the manner of amusing children's cartoons, choosing instead children's Bibles that retell and illustrate the stories more realistically.

Choose a Children's Bible That Agrees with Your Theological Perspective and Values

A fourth approach some take is simply to choose a children's Bible that is not necessarily a completely objective adaptation but one that seems consistent with their own beliefs and values. Socially conservative evangelical Christians, then, may choose *The Right Choices Bible*[13] by evangelical Christian authors Dottie McDowell and Josh McDowell or the *Focus on the Family Bedtime Bible*.[14] Conversely, more moderate or progressive Christians may choose children's Bibles such as Archbishop Desmond Tutu's *Children of God Storybook Bible*,[15] Alice Bach and J. Cheryl Exum's *Moses' Ark: Stories from the Bible*,[16] or Elizabeth F. Caldwell and Carol A. Wehrheim's *Growing in God's Love: A Story Bible*,[17] which highlight the Bible's themes of social justice and inclusion.[18] Still others may choose children's Bibles that are created and published by members of their own religious sect or denomination. Those who take this approach, however, may still want to explain to their children that the children's Bible they are reading is not the Bible itself but rather a retelling of the Bible's stories from a particular viewpoint.

Conclusion

Which approach to children's Bibles is best for you and your children? The information presented here is not intended to dictate a particular approach to children's Bibles or to recommend a specific children's Bible. In consultation with their children, each parent, caregiver, and religious educator needs to consider which approach, and perhaps which children's Bibles, are best for them.

Questions for Discussion

1. What Bible story books or children's Bibles do you own? What have you noticed about the way they adapt the Bible's stories?

2. Dalton mentions several approaches to choosing children's Bibles and other Bibles for children. Which approach do you use or do you most resonate with? Why? What other approaches, if any, do you use?

3. In what ways can we partner with children to read and understand Bible stories in age-appropriate ways?

4. What are the values by which we can determine if a children's Bible is a good fit for our church or family? How can we interrogate and challenge messages in children's Bibles that may not match our personal beliefs?

Notes

1. Carolyn Larsen, *Little Girls Bible Storybook for Mothers and Daughters*, illustrated by Caron Turk (Grand Rapids, MI: Baker, 1998), 24–30.

2. As a result of this, I ended up writing a book and several articles and essays on children's Bibles. I will cite some of these at relevant points throughout this essay for those who are interested in exploring matters in more detail.

3. For more details and examples, see Russell W. Dalton, "Children's Bibles in the United States," in *The Oxford Handbook of the Bible in America*, ed. Paul C. Guthjahr (Cambridge: Oxford University Press, 2017), 25–34.

4. For a more in-depth discussion, see Russell W. Dalton, *Children's Bibles in America: A Reception History of the Story of Noah's Ark in U.S. Children's Bibles* (London: Bloomsbury, 2015), 99–115.

5. See Russell W. Dalton, "Emerging Trends in Christian Children's Bibles in the United States," in *The Bible in American Life*, ed. Philip Goff et al. (Cambridge: Oxford University Press, 2017), 228–30.

6. See David Gunn, "Cultural Criticism," in *Judges and Method: New Approaches in Biblical Studies*, ed. Gale A. Yee, 2nd ed. (Minneapolis: Fortress, 2007), 205–7.

7. For more examples and details, see Russell W. Dalton, "Perfect Prophets, Helpful Hippos and Happy Endings: Noah and Jonah in Children's Bible Storybooks in the U.S.," *Religious Education* 102, no. 3 (June 2007): 305.

8. For examples, see *Children of Color Storybook Bible* (Nashville: Thomas Nelson, 2001); Desmond Tutu, *Children of God Storybook Bible* (Grand Rapids, MI: Zonderkidz, 2010); and Elizabeth F. Caldwell and Carol A. Wehrheim, eds., *Growing in God's Love: A Story Bible* (Louisville: Westminster John Knox, 2018).

9. Ronald Goldman, *Readiness for Religion: A Basis for Developmental Religious Education* (New York: Seabury, 1965), 71.

10. See, e.g., Reedsy Ltd., "125 Best Children's Books of All-Time," accessed June 9, 2023, https://reedsy.com/discovery/blog/best-childrens-books; and Mary Harris Russell, "CC Recommends," accessed August 24, 2023, https://www.christiancentury.org/reviews/2007-12/cc-recommends-2.

11. See Ruth B. Bottigheimer, "The Otherness of Children's Bibles in Historical Perspective," in Caroline Vander Stichele and Hugh S. Pyper, eds., *Text, Image, and Otherness in Children's Bibles: What Is in the Picture?* (Atlanta: Society of Biblical Literature, 2012), 321.

12. See, e.g., *The Children's Bible* (New York: Golden Press, 1962); Sandol Stoddard, *The BOMC Illustrated Children's Bible* (New York: Book of the Month Club, 2001); Ann Pilling, *The Kingfisher Children's Bible*, illustrated by Kady MacDonald Denton (New York: Kingfisher, 1993); and Selina Hastings, *The Children's Illustrated Bible*, illustrated by Eric Thomas (New York: Dorling Kindersley, 1994).

13. Dottie McDowell and Josh McDowell, *The Right Choices Bible*, illustrated by Joe Boddy (Wheaton, IL: Tyndale, 1998).

14. Rick Osborne, Mary Guenther, and K. Christie Bowler, *Focus on the Family Bedtime Bible* (Wheaton, IL: Tyndale, 2002).

15. Tutu, *Children of God Storybook Bible*.

16. Alice Bach and J. Cheryl Exum, *Moses' Ark*, illustrated by Leo Dillon and Diane Dillon (New York: Delacorte, 1989).

17. Caldwell and Wehrheim, *Growing in God's Love*.

18. For examples of how children's Bibles often obscure themes of justice, see Dalton, "Meek and Mild: American Children's Bibles' Stories of Jesus as a Boy," *Religious Education* 109, no. 1 (2014): 45–60.

References

Bach, Alice, and J. Cheryl Exum. *Moses' Ark*. Illustrated by Leo Dillon and Diane Dillon. New York: Delacorte, 1989.

Bottigheimer, Ruth B. "The Otherness of Children's Bibles in Historical Perspective." In *Text, Image, and Otherness in Children's Bibles: What Is in the Picture?*, edited by Caroline Vander Stichele and Hugh S. Pyper, 321–32. Atlanta: Society of Biblical Literature, 2012.

Caldwell, Elizabeth F., and Carol A. Wehrheim, eds. *Growing in God's Love: A Story Bible*. Louisville: Westminster John Knox, 2018.

Children of Color Storybook Bible. Illustrated by Victor Hogan. Nashville: Thomas Nelson, 2001.

The Children's Bible. New York: Golden Press, 1962.

Dalton, Russell W. *Children's Bibles in America: A Reception History of the Story of Noah's Ark in U.S. Children's Bibles*. London: Bloomsbury, 2015.

———. "Children's Bibles in the United States." In *The Oxford Handbook of the Bible in America*, edited by Paul C. Guthjahr, 25–34. Cambridge: Oxford University Press, 2017.

———. "Emerging Trends in Christian Children's Bibles in the United States." In *The Bible in American Life*, edited by Philip Goff et al., 228–30. New York: Oxford University Press, 2017.

———. "Meek and Mild: American Children's Bibles' Stories of Jesus as a Boy." *Religious Education* 109, no. 1 (2014): 45–60.

———. "Perfect Prophets, Helpful Hippos and Happy Endings: Noah and Jonah in Children's Bible Storybooks in the U.S." *Religious Education* 102, no. 3 (June 2007): 305.

Goldman, Ronald. *Readiness for Religion: A Basis for Developmental Religious Education*. New York: Seabury, 1965.

Gunn, David. "Cultural Criticism." In *Judges and Method: New Approaches in Biblical Studies*, edited by Gale A. Yee, 2nd ed., 205–7. Minneapolis: Fortress, 2007.

Hastings, Selina. *The Children's Illustrated Bible*. Illustrated by Eric Thomas. New York: Dorling Kindersley, 1994.

Larsen, Carolyn. *Little Girls Bible Storybook for Mothers and Daughters*. Illustrated by Caron Turk. Grand Rapids, MI: Baker, 1998.

McDowell, Dottie, and Josh McDowell. *The Right Choices Bible*. Illustrated by Joe Boddy. Wheaton, IL: Tyndale, 1998.

Osborne, Rick, Mary Guenther, and K. Christie Bowler. *Focus on the Family Bedtime Bible*. Wheaton, IL: Tyndale, 2002.

Pilling, Ann. *The Kingfisher Children's Bible*. Illustrated by Kady MacDonald Denton. New York: Kingfisher, 1993.

Reedsy Ltd. "125 Best Children's Books of All-Time." Accessed June 9, 2023. https://reedsy.com/discovery/blog/best-childrens-books.

Russell, Mary Harris. "CC Recommends." Accessed August 24, 2023. https://www.christiancentury.org/reviews/2007-12/cc-recommends-2.

Stoddard, Sandol. *The BOMC Illustrated Children's Bible*. New York: Book of the Month Club, 2001.

Tutu, Desmond. *Children of God Storybook Bible*. Grand Rapids, MI: Zonderkidz, 2010.

3

Choosing Books for Children

VIRGINIA A. LEE

Children's books are important for a variety of reasons. Books help children learn listening skills and new words. They also expand a child's vocabulary, building empathy and emotional awareness while providing bonding with parents and caregivers who read to them.[1] Books help children increase their attention span, spark their creativity, learn life lessons, and help with social and emotional development.[2]

Stories are one of six tools that religious educator Tanya Eustace Campen identifies that families can use "to engage God's presence and love."[3] "When families gather to read, share, watch, or experience a story together, we enter a holy moment of wonder and discovery, a moment to which we come with curiosity and wonder. We come with a willingness to learn and discover together. We set aside the need to provide the answers."[4]

Books help children begin to understand themselves and their world through the stories they tell.

Since children's books are so important, how can we make good decisions and choices when selecting them? The following articles inform the choices for texts and resources I use for seminary courses. They might also provide guidance for selecting children's books. They are "Curriculum as Window and Mirror"[5] by Emily Style, "Mirrors, Windows, and Sliding Glass Doors"[6] by Rudine Sims Bishop, and "Why Stop at Windows and Mirrors? Children's Books Prisms"[7] by Uma Krishnaswami.

In a 1988 article, Emily Style explored the concept of windows and mirrors as a necessary curriculum component. "[There is a] need for curriculum to function both as window and mirror, in order to reflect and reveal most accurately both a multicultural world and the student [themselves]. If the student is understood as occupying a dwelling of self, education needs to enable the student to look through window frames in order to see the realities of others and into mirrors in order to see [their] own reality reflected."[8]

Style also noted another important point that Krishnaswami expands further in her article. Using a narrative poem, she illustrated that while everyone may look through the same window (of the poem), they do not all see the same thing because "their knowledge is detached and objective."[9]

In 1988 both secular educational curricula and religious education resources provided many mirrors for white men to see themselves reflected in the curriculum while providing few windows to learn about other perspectives. Women and Black, Indigenous, People of Color (BIPOC) seldom saw themselves reflected in the resources, while always having to look through windows. While in seminary in the late 1980s, I became aware of the multitude of women's stories that I had not heard while in elementary and high school, college, or Sunday school.

Lest you think that this could not possibly be a problem in this century, I wrote about another aspect of curriculum in 2014, dealing with how women and girls are portrayed:

> I must admit that it [still] surprises me that . . . women are still ignored and still invisible in many places. As I write this article, Dick's Sporting Goods is dealing with the public relations problems related to a letter from a 12-year-old girl/

athlete who asked where the girl athletes were in their most recent catalog. In 2014, a store can produce a catalog and not include any female athletes, and no one notices until a 12-year-old brings it to their attention. In this catalog, women watch sports from the sidelines and grandstands rather than play sports. The message seems to be quite clear; women are spectators and not athletes. Women . . . often find curriculum that functions as windows on new worlds, but have difficulty finding mirrors that reflect their own experience.[10]

Several years after Style's article, Rudine Sims Bishop helpfully expanded the metaphor:

> Books are sometimes windows, offering views of worlds that may be real or imagined, familiar or strange. These windows are also sliding glass doors, and readers have only to walk through in imagination to become part of whatever world has been created and recreated by the author. When lighting conditions are just right, however, a window can also be a mirror. Literature transforms human experience and reflects it back to us, and in that reflection we can see our own lives and experiences as part of the larger human experience. Reading, then, becomes a means of self-affirmation, and readers often seek their mirrors in books.[11]

When children step through the sliding glass door and experience a new world through the eyes of that author, children learn about new perspectives and possibilities. And when they can see themselves reflected in the books they read, they understand that they are valued also.

In 2019 Uma Krishnaswami revisited the windows and mirror metaphor. While acknowledging the helpfulness of the metaphor, Krishnaswami also realized that the metaphors did not work for all communities. "For example, applying the window image to Native American stories, educator Debbie Reese calls for a curtain: 'Native communities resisted historical oppression and continue to preserve our culture by cultivating our ways in private spaces—behind the curtain. While Native people share some of our ways publicly in the present day, there is a great deal that we continue to protect from outsiders.' A window lets you look into a space other than the one you occupy, but (as Reese implies) what does it do to me to be the object of your gaze?"[12] With this information and her own experience in writing children's books, Krishnaswami considered how books might function as prisms that can change our expectations. "A prism can slow and bend the light that passes through it, splitting that light into component colors. It can refract light in as many directions as the prism's shape and surface planes allow. Similarly, books can disrupt and challenge ideas about diversity through multifaceted and intersecting characters at these crucial intersections and give them power to reframe their stories. Through the fictional world, they can make us question the assumptions and practices of our own real world."[13]

These three articles are reminders to me each semester when I choose texts for my seminary courses. Do the textbooks provide mirrors for all students to see themselves? Do textbooks provide opportunities for students to look beyond themselves and learn about new ideas and perspectives? Do textbooks provide prisms where students' ideas are challenged or disrupted and where they must use critical thinking skills to challenge their assumptions? These are good questions to use when choosing children's books also.

In 2016 my colleague Dr. Reginald Blount and I helped to establish the Garrett-Evanston Children's Defense Fund (CDF) Freedom Schools program, which was a collaboration of Garrett-Evangelical Theological Seminary, the City of Evanston, School District 65, and many faith communities. CDF Freedom Schools programs help children fall in love with reading. For many scholars (what children are called in Freedom Schools), an outcome of attendance is that it can help prevent the summer reading slide. A hallmark of the program is the library of books. Each classroom has a library of books, and there is a communal library for each Freedom School. Scholars spend the morning reading and learning critical reading skills. Everyone in the building reads for fifteen minutes during DEAR (Drop Everything And Read) time. Each scholar takes home a book a week for six weeks. All the books are culturally relevant for the scholars in the program. This is another way of saying that the selected books provide mirrors in which children see themselves in the books they read. As Rudine Sims Bishop notes above, when children can see their own experience reflected in a book, reading becomes a means of affirmation. We witnessed the difference this affirmation made for scholars in the program. Scholars who entered on the first day believing they could not read left knowing that they could read and believing they could make a difference in themselves, their families, their communities, and the world.[14]

When choosing culturally relevant books, we must also consider the concept of cultural authenticity and who gets to tell whose story. The author of a book makes many choices in how they portray children and their cultural context. I spent my childhood on a dairy farm in rural Virginia, and I can still remember how frustrated I was when someone who had never lived on a farm thought they could tell me what really happened on farms. Most of the time, they were completely wrong! Their assumptions were not very helpful in talking about a context they had not experienced.

Cultural authenticity in children's books is a highly debated concept. *Stories Matter: The Complexity of Cultural Authenticity in Children's Literature* contains more than twenty articles by diverse authors with different perspectives. Even the definition of cultural authenticity is contested in this book. Rudine Sims Bishop can be helpful here also. She argues that "cultural authenticity cannot be defined, although 'you know it when you see it' as an insider reading a book about your own culture."[15] E. F. Howard defines cultural authenticity by saying that "we cannot ignore what the book does to the reader . . . and . . . that we know a book is 'true' because we feel it deep down, saying, 'Yes, that's how it is.'"[16]

I find myself agreeing with Jaqueline Woodson, whose chapter in *Stories Matter* is titled "Who Can Tell My Story?"[17] She explains that people often write about other contexts and cultures they may have seen through a window, looking into the house, but they have never been inside the house. Seeing through that window might expose someone to new ideas, concepts, and perspectives, but it does not give an insider's view of the context.

A good example of this can be seen in a review of the book *My Heart Is on the Ground: The Diary of Nannie Little Rose, a Sioux Girl, Carlisle Indian School, Pennsylvania, 1880*.[18] Although the book is written as if it is a Native American child's real diary, it is fictional. The book is a part of the Dear America series, and it has received favorable reviews in *School Library Journal* and *Booklist*.[19] The nine women authors of the review include research specialists and Native American teachers and learners. While the review notes appropriation (the title is from a Cheyenne proverb),[20] lack of historical accuracy (numerous examples),[21] and stereotypes (regarding language and derogatory references to girls),[22] the review includes over four pages of "lack of cultural authenticity."[23] All those examples make clear that the person writing the book is an "outsider" to the culture and misunderstands many aspects of the culture, regardless of the research they might have done.

For this reason, I look for books written by persons who know a context, community, or event through their participation in or experience with that context. I want children to see themselves accurately portrayed so they may recognize themselves in that mirror, and I want children looking through a window or sliding glass door into a new and different perspective to hear and see from an "insider." Another reason I do this is to support publishing diverse perspectives in children's books.

In 1985 fewer than 1 percent of children's books spotlighted Black characters. Twenty years later, not much had changed. In 2015 children were about five times more likely to encounter a talking truck or dinosaur on the page than a Hispanic character. By 2019 more than 12 percent of US-published children's books featured Black characters, according to the University of Wisconsin's Cooperative Children's Book Center. Additionally, 9 percent of books featured Asian characters, 6.3 percent featured Hispanic characters, and less than 1 percent had Native American or Alaska Native characters. While children's books still are not as diverse as the children who read them, progress is being made.[24]

While these numbers are increasing, the percentages are still too small. And not all books that feature diverse characters are written by authors from the same context. The website "We Need Diverse Books" is a great place to explore more of these concepts and to find a variety of diverse books.[25] The Cooperative Children's Book Center (CCBC) at the University of Wisconsin–Madison provides helpful diversity statistics for children's books.[26]

So why are diverse books important in raising faithful children? First, all children are created in the image of God and should be able to see themselves reflected and affirmed in the books they read. In the first book in this series, *Raising Faithful Kids: This Is the Stuff of Faith*, Erin S. Keyes noted that a child in her class did not believe they could accomplish what the children in the book had accomplished. When she asked why, he said because there was no one in the book who looked like him.[27] Second, books reflect our values and beliefs. Compassion, empathy, care, concern, and hospitality are just a few of the values that are important for our children to know and practice, and we can reflect those values in the books we choose.

So how do we choose the best books for our children? I suggest beginning with the following questions when choosing a book. Every book does not need to meet every category, but children need to have access to books in all categories—mirrors, windows, and prisms. This list is not exhaustive, but it is a place to begin.

- Is this a book where children can see themselves accurately represented (culture, gender, sexuality, family structure, race, religious affiliation, etc.)? Note that this means that not all children will be reflected in all books. That is why a home, school, or faith community library needs to have a variety of diverse books.
- Does this book represent the diversity of God's creation?
- Does this book help children look through a window to learn something new or to see a new perspective?
- Does this book help children step through the sliding glass door to enter a new world that might be different from their own?
- Does this book reflect a context different from my child's context?
- Does this book help create prisms that may disrupt or challenge one's thinking, ones that help children question their assumptions, which is the beginning of thinking critically?
- Is the book written by persons who are a part of the story they are telling?
- Does the book represent Native American peoples today? There is a tendency to talk, speak, and write about Native American peoples in the past tense as if they no longer exist.[28]
- Does this book fill a space, category, or perspective that is missing in my child's library?

Another way to choose diverse books is to get to know some good resources that curate good lists. Here are some of my favorites. This is certainly not an exhaustive list; it is just a beginning. I hope that it will lead you to other helpful sites.

- Read Across America website[29] (and their Tune into KidLit TV, which is a "read-aloud" program that "brings authors' voices into the classroom."[30])
- We Need Diverse Books[31]
- Rebekah Gienapp's website, which includes numerous booklists on a variety of topics and anti-racism resources for children[32]
- American Indians in children's books[33]
- Social Justice Books, which includes a "Guide for Selecting Anti-Bias Children's Books"[34]
- The Conscious Kid, which includes "read-aloud" with authors[35]
- Welcoming Schools Diverse Picture Books with Transgender, Non-Binary, and Gender Expansive Characters list[36]
- Netflix—search for "Bookmarks: Celebrating Black Voices," which includes authors reading their books

As the children, grandchildren, and great-nieces and great-nephews of educators, all of my great-nieces and great-nephews have overflowing bookshelves. They already love books, and they currently have or have had a ritual of reading with one of their parents each night. I hope those books provide a glimpse into the wonder and diversity of God's creation and also affirm their value in their home and faith communities.

Questions for Discussion

1. Lee shows in this chapter the importance of choosing a curriculum for children. What does your faith community do to ensure diversity is represented in the curriculum, and how are children represented in the curriculum?
2. Does your church have a library accessible to children and adults alike? Evaluate your inventory of books. How does it respond to some of the questions raised in the article?

3. Do the books you have in your home reflect the values you want to represent?
4. Do the books in your home library or faith community library provide windows, mirrors, and prisms for all children? What books might you need to add?

Notes

1. "Why It Is Important to Read to Your Child," Child Mind Institute, accessed November 3, 2023, https://childmind.org/article/why-is-it-important-to-read-to-your-child/.

2. "Reading to Children: Why It's So Important and How to Start," Healthline, accessed November 3, 2023, https://www.healthline.com/health/childrens-health/reading-to-children#when-and-how-to-start.

3. Tanya Marie Eustace Campen, "Holy Work with Families: Living Out Our Faith Together," in *Let the Children Lead: Exploring Children's Spirituality Today*, ed. Elizabeth DeGaynor (Alexandria, VA: VTS Press, 2023), 66–67.

4. Campen, "Holy Work with Families," 67.

5. Emily Style, "Curriculum as Window and Mirror," SEED, 1988, accessed November 3, 2023, https://nationalseedproject.org/Key-SEED-Texts/curriculum-as-window-and-mirror.

6. Rudine Sims Bishop, "Mirrors, Windows, and Sliding Glass Doors," January 3, 2015, Reading Is Fundamental, https://scenicregional.org/wp-content/uploads/2017/08/Mirrors-Windows-and-Sliding-Glass-Doors.pdf. Originally published in *Perspectives: Choosing and Using Books for the Classroom* 6, no. 3 (Summer 1990).

7. Uma Krishnaswami, "Why Stop at Windows and Mirrors? Children's Books Prisms," *The Horn Book Magazine* 95, no. 1 (January–February 2019): 54–59.

8. Style, "Curriculum as Window and Mirror." Text modified for inclusive language.

9. Style, "Curriculum as Window and Mirror."

10. Virginia Lee, "My United Methodist Perspective of 'Core' Curriculum," *Religious Education* 110, no. 1 (2015): 24–27, https://doi.org/10.1080/00344087.2015.989093.

11. Bishop, "Mirrors, Windows, and Sliding Glass Doors."

12. Krishnaswami, "Why Stop at Windows and Mirrors?"

13. Krishnaswami, "Why Stop at Windows and Mirrors?"

14. For more information about CDF Freedom Schools programs see https://www.childrensdefense.org/programs/cdf-freedom-schools/.

15. Kathy G. Short and Dana L. Fox, "The Complexity of Cultural Authenticity in Children's Literature: Why the Debates Really Matter," in *Stories Matter: The Complexity of Cultural Authenticity in Children's Literature*, ed. Kathy G. Short and Dana L. Fox (Urbana, IL: National Council of Teachers of English, 2003), 4.

16. Cited in Short and Fox, "The Complexity of Cultural Authenticity in Children's Literature," 5.

17. Jacquelin Woodson, "Who Can Tell My Story?" in *Stories Matter: The Complexity of Cultural Authenticity in Children's Literature*, ed. Kathy G. Short and Dana L. Fox (Urbana, IL: National Council of Teachers of English, 2003), 41–45.

18. Doris Seale and Beverly Slapin, eds., *A Broken Flute: The Native Experience in Books for Children* (Berkeley, CA: Oyate, 2005).

19. "My Heart Is on the Ground and the Indian Residential School Experience," in *A Broken Flute: The Native Experience in Books for Children*, ed. Doris Seale and Beverly Slapin (Berkeley, CA: Oyate, 2005), 61.

20. "My Heart Is on the Ground and the Indian Residential School Experience," 61.

21. "My Heart Is on the Ground and the Indian Residential School Experience," 62.

22. "My Heart Is on the Ground and the Indian Residential School Experience," 67–68.

23. "My Heart Is on the Ground and the Indian Residential School Experience," 63–67.

24. Mary Ellen Flannery, "Why We Need Diverse Books," NeaToday, October 26, 2020, https://www.nea.org/nea-today/all-news-articles/why-we-need-diverse-books.

25. WNDB (We Need Diverse Books), accessed November 9, 2023, https://diversebooks.org/.

26. Kari Dickinson, "CCBC's Latest Diversity Statistics Show Increasing Number of Diverse Books for Children and Teens," University of Wisconsin–Madison School of Education, June 13, 2023, https://education.wisc.edu/news/ccbcs-latest-diversity-statistics-show-increasing-number-of-diverse-books-for-children-and-teens/.

27. Erin S. Keyes, "Teaching by What We Leave Out," in *Raising Faithful Kids: This Is the Stuff of Faith*, ed. Denise Janssen, Carmichael Crutchfield, Virginia A. Lee, and Jessica Young Brown (Valley Forge, PA: Judson Press, 2024), 106–107.

28. American Indians in Children's Literature, accessed November 9, 2023, https://americanindiansinchildrensliterature.blogspot.com/.

29. Read Across America, NEA, accessed November 9, 2023, https://www.nea.org/professional-excellence/student-engagement/read-across-america.

30. "Tune into KidLit TV," KidLit TV, accessed November 9, 2023, https://www.nea.org/professional-excellence/student-engagement/read-across-america/support-your-readers/tune-into-kidlit-tv.

31. WNDB.

32. Rebekah Gienapp, accessed November 9, 2023, https://www.rebekahgienapp.com/.

33. American Indians in Children's Literature, accessed November 9, 2023, https://americanindiansinchildrensliterature.blogspot.com/.

34. Louise Derman-Sparks, "Guide for Selecting Anti-Bias Children's Books," Social Justice Books, accessed November 9, 2023, https://socialjusticebooks.org/guide-for-selecting-anti-bias-childrens-books/.

35. "The Conscious Kid Story Time," The Conscious Kid, accessed November 9, 2023, https://www.theconsciouskid.org/storytime.

36. "Diverse Picture Books with Transgender, Non-Binary and Gender Expansive Characters," Welcoming Schools, accessed November 9, 2023, https://assets2.hrc.org/welcoming-schools/documents/WS_Diverse_Picture_Books_Transgender_Non-Binary.pdf.

4

Keeping the End in Mind

DENISE JANSSEN

It was a warm summer evening in the Marshall home, but the icy silence betrayed the season. Amanda sat on the porch swing, struggling to hold back her tears as she silently wondered why it felt like her family was falling apart. Ryan and Lily, now fourteen and seventeen, barely spoke when they were home, mostly limiting their communication to monosyllabic responses and requests for money or permission to go out. She could not talk with Michael, their father, about their lack of communication. He would not discuss it. He was sure the kids' willfulness and disrespect were the issue, that Amanda was too lenient with them. Tears fell as she remembered sweet moments with her babies, reading stories and cuddling together at bedtime. Amanda was concerned that she could barely get them to go to church with the family anymore, much less care about the faith she and Michael raised them in. This certainly was not the way she hoped her children would turn out. Sure, she and Michael had made some mistakes as parents. 'What did we know about raising children except how we were raised?' she pondered. She wanted their relationships to be better, but Amanda had no idea where to begin.

Parents and caregivers sometimes picture adolescence in their minds as something akin to an impending storm. Perhaps this idea comes from stories they hear from others' families or the media, or maybe they remember their own bumpy adolescence or that of their peers, fraught with frustration and disillusionment. What may be an irrational fear can be all too real as parents and caregivers imagine that one day their sweet little child will wake up an adolescent, someone they no longer understand, a volatile person they fear to be filled with angst, insolence, and hormones. What's more, some parents and caregivers also fear—for good reason—that their child who looks older than their years will be mistaken for dangerous or violent with all the baggage our culture imputes. Memories of snuggles, songs, and bedtime prayers give way to the unknown as this developmental transition unfolds.

Though these fears about the transition to adolescence are rooted in some reality, the children we have known show more continuity than disruption as they transition to adolescence. Many of the same principles of relational parenting and caregiving that create healthy relationships in a child's early life remain agile and effective as those relationships shift in the adolescent years. So too, many of the practices whereby parents/caregivers and children form faith together remain helpful and effective into adolescence. Simply put, parents/caregivers need not let negative cultural narratives or fears impede their own positive relationships with their children as they grow through adolescence and into adulthood.

Beginning with the End in Mind

Curriculum development has a principle—backward design—that I find helpful as a metaphor for thinking about the continuum of raising faithful kids. Backward design draws on a concept offered by motivational speaker and business consultant Stephen Covey in the 1980s, wherein he noted that having the intended result in mind allows the steps along the way to be more strategic. The principle in its simplest form is this: Begin with the end in mind.[1] If we do not have a vision of the end product we hope to achieve, we cannot make strategic and well-informed decisions that will contribute to achieving that goal. With a clear sense of the hoped-for outcome, we can make choices from the start that will build toward the vision we have.

I do not intend to compare raising children to running a business, but I suggest the concept of backward design holds wisdom for us as we make parenting and caregiving choices when children are very young. Those foundational choices will help us realize our vision for who we will be together in the future, for the kinds of relationships we will have in adolescence and adulthood. Because forming faith is something we engage in together with children throughout our lives, beginning with the end in mind contributes to the formation of a durable and agile faith for them and us.

The End We Have in Mind

What do we hope for the children for whom we care? What qualities and values do we hope for them to have as adults? What vision do we have, and how do we begin to share in forming and living into that vision as children grow and have a greater sense of agency? These questions are less about specifics like what children will do for their work or what they will choose to value and where they direct their energy. More so, I mean "the end we have in mind" in a general sense of qualities and traits that are broadly shared—things like agency, bodily autonomy, healthy boundaries, a value on meaning-making in faith formation, and the ability to self-regulate, to name a few. In a sense, these are tools caregivers can help children gain to form a tool kit that will serve them well in adulthood.

In the beginning . . .

For caregivers and parents just embarking on this journey, adolescence or adulthood can feel like the distant future when they look at their precious little one. But it is critical to remember that this is the beginning of a relationship with a tiny human being who will someday be an adult. This relationship is a continuum that builds on prior experiences and interactions. Who we are with the children we love when they are young becomes incorporated into who we will be together as they grow, though it will certainly morph and change. The choices we make in our interactions with children become layered over the years, understood and remembered from the perspective of the unique human beings we are, and form the stuff of our relationships together.

In considering the end we have in mind—the tool kit we hope to help children develop that will equip them well into adulthood—we can focus and ground our choices in parenting and caregiving. Thinking of future implications raises our awareness of the reality that the small and seemingly insignificant choices and interactions we have with children matter more than may seem to be the case. Beginning with the end in mind helps us to pay attention to these choices and interactions from the start. Here are a few examples.[2]

Agency

If we hope for the children in our care to have a sense of agency in adulthood, we need to pay attention to our choices as their primary caregivers to protect that sense of agency and keep it intact. This might mean taking care to give children choices only when they are real choices (instead of "What would you like for dinner?" offer options from among what is available). Giving a child choices involves ensuring that a child has a say in what they will do or not do. Pausing to help a child be ready for something they need to endure for their own good (like an inoculation) will help the child learn coping strategies that reduce trauma and serve them well into adulthood. Even something as simple as a parent picking up a small child can be an opportunity for the child to have a say in the matter. Even when picking them up is necessary for their safety, the child can be given an opportunity to understand that it is necessary. This does not mean there are no limits or rules, nor are children given all the power. Rather, I simply mean to acknowledge that they have some power, and that power begins with agency over some of their choices.

Protecting our children's sense of agency is important in faith formation, as well. If attending church services and activities is something we value for our children, giving children choices about how they will participate helps to keep a child's sense of agency intact. Hearing them when they feel uncomfortable about a person, setting, or activity is crucial, as well. Faith language is often figurative and metaphorical, and children tend to understand things in more literal or tangible terms, which makes wondering together and allowing space for the mysteries of faith helpful. Too often faith formation with children is moralizing, as in *Aesop's Fables*, rather than focusing on making meaning together. Adults do not need to have all the answers to wonder together or make meaning with their children in day-to-day life. Further, children are capable of making meaning of life experiences through the lens of faith and choosing helpful ways of expressing their faith with the partnership of their primary adults. The important adults in their children's lives can support them in expressing their faith by modeling and discussing with children how and why they, as adults, make their choices and make meaning of their actions. Protecting children's agency to choose about faith as they are developmentally able at each stage of growth is a way caregivers and parents can support children.

Bodily Autonomy

If we want children to have bodily autonomy when they become adolescents and adults and make healthy choices about sharing their bodies, we could take the extra step to ask to touch them (or let them know something needs to happen and give them some time to feel ready to allow it). As caregivers, supporting autonomy might also mean helping well-meaning relatives and friends to understand that the child is free to decide if they want to hug or kiss or if another expression is more comfortable. Reinforcing children's choices in this area can help them feel more confident in naming those choices and expecting others to honor them. If the child feels a sense of ownership of their body, and if we as parents and caregivers help to protect their sense of ownership, then as children grow into adolescence and beyond, they will more clearly understand that they have the right to say no to unwanted touch and expect to be respected by others.

In terms of faith formation, supporting autonomy can mean helping children anticipate what to expect in a public worship space and giving them acceptable choices about how they will interact. It might mean practicing ahead of time at home so children can anticipate how particular practices will make them feel and how they will respond, such as the pastor touching their head or shoulder to offer a blessing or the priest putting the Communion wafer in their mouth. Helping children to listen to their own inner voice when it comes to setting boundaries about their bodies builds the confidence they need now and in the future.

Beginning with the end in mind means preserving a child's sense of bodily autonomy so they grow through adolescence and into adulthood with a healthy body image and an understanding that choices about their body are theirs to make. Later in life, our children will likely feel confident making good decisions about their bodies, even when those decisions are difficult or uncomfortable.

Self-Regulation

Caregivers and parents can help children deal with big feelings by modeling with their own behavior and words. Too often grown-ups get away with behaving in ways we would never allow our children to behave: hitting when angry, demanding behavior that negates the autonomy of others, breaking rules and then denying it, and causing hurt without apologizing.

Because adults are larger and more powerful, and because children are dependent on their caregivers and parents, they can be the victims of adults' bullying and hurtful behaviors with no recourse. This is why self-regulation on the part of parents and caregivers is essential as a matter of integrity and modeling healthy practices for the children we love.

When children are "throwing a tantrum" or "misbehaving," adults too often label it as bad behavior in need of punishment. Children encounter feelings like joy, sadness, hurt, pain, frustration, and embarrassment just as adults do, but children are still learning how to recognize these feelings, express them in helpful ways, and take steps to deal with them. Frequently the only models children have are grown-ups who may not have had good role models and have not learned how to constructively deal with their own big feelings. The same behaviors parents get away with are disciplined in children, which leads to anger and distrust as adolescent sensitivity to hypocrisy rises. Taking responsibility for self-regulating as adults means beginning with the end in mind, taking the time to learn to talk about big feelings—ours and our children's—and deal with them in healthy ways from the start.

The faith value of seeking and giving forgiveness is helpful here. Amish Christians have a practice of intentionally asking forgiveness of their children, modeling this behavior, and allowing forgiveness to become a way of life. The practice of genuinely seeking forgiveness—saying and hearing the words "I'm sorry," and hearing or saying "I forgive you"—is deeply healing to relationships. When we begin with the end in mind, we remember that it is worth the investment of an extra few minutes and a bit of our pride since the relationships we build with our children are lifelong and formative.

. . . With the End in Mind

Faith formation with children is a continuum. Human beings are constantly building on prior experiences and knowledge as they develop in complexity and capacity. Faith formation is part of this and involves a relationship with God and relationships with people, especially the most important people in children's lives: caregivers and parents. Our relationships with our children from the very beginning through adulthood are layered with words, actions, and experiences, including the way we make each other feel and who we tell each other we are, both explicitly and implicitly. The end we have in mind—the relationship we hope to have with our adolescent and adult children—begins in infancy and builds through all our interactions. Thus, years of unacknowledged pain and hurts that have gone without apology add up. So much about how childhood typically unfolds removes a child's sense of agency (think about public education and what the messages "doing what you're told" and "because I said so" send). Faith formation filled with childhood wonder and mystery is a great way to practice agency together.

Forming faith with children means helping them make their own meaning, enabling children to choose faith practices that build a durable and agile faith that will serve them well throughout their lives. Fostering agency throughout childhood can help ease the shift into adolescence when claiming agency can feel like rebellion. If we acknowledge our children's agency all along, this shift into adolescence can feel less disjunctive and disruptive. In reality adolescent and adult children still need their parents' love and help. By paying attention to and taking steps to foster relationships throughout childhood, we create space for relationships to grow and change through adolescence and into adulthood.

Grace Abounds: A Word for Parents and Caregivers Who Need a Do-Over

Let's face it—the process of child-rearing can be overwhelming. Life is stressful, and raising children can amplify that stress. And children do not come with a manual to help us know how to do this parenting/caregiving thing right! Parents and caregivers are under a lot of pressure culturally to have all the answers. Advice about raising children is big business: Consider the thousands of books shelved in public libraries and bookstores with competing strategies and values. Regardless of what you may have learned when you were growing up, parents and caregivers do not have all the answers, and they do not have to have all the answers.

Our faith has a message for all of us imperfect parents and caregivers: Simply put, grace abounds! If you know of ways you have already messed up or things you wish you could go back and do over, there is no better time than the present to turn things around. Children are predisposed to love you, to be on your side, and to cheer for you. Often they are more ready to forgive than we are to ask. Children can work together to change an unhelpful practice or rebuild trust and relationships. Forgiveness helps to make meaning of a hurtful experience. Behavior that is respectable, like admitting fault and asking forgiveness, begets respect and builds relationships that grow, change, and last. Parents and caregivers can begin again in their relationships with children—begin again with the end in mind of a lifelong loving relationship.

Do you remember the initial story of Amanda and her family? She and Michael are learning new practices and values as they grow in their relationship with their two children. May the same be true for us all.

Questions for Discussion

1. What "end" have we envisioned for the children we are charged with? What qualities do we hope they will possess in adulthood?

2. What practices can help us to slow down enough to consider the end during challenging caregiving moments?

3. How can we offer ourselves and others grace while caregiving?

Notes

1. Grant Wiggins and Jay McTighe, *Understanding by Design* (Alexandria, VA: Association for Supervision and Curriculum Development, 2005).

2. Ideas that follow are drawn broadly from the body of childist literature emerging from the work of the Childism Institute at Rutgers University. For more information and a bibliography of resources, visit childism.org.

5

"And I Am Way More"

TAMAR WASOIAN

While preparing for lunch, I overheard the children in my three-year-old preschool classroom discussing if stealing is right or wrong.

>   CHILD 1: Is stealing wrong?
>   CHILD 2: Yes, my daddy said stealing is wrong.
>   CHILD 1: But Robin Hood was stealing and sharing. My dad said sharing is good.

They continued discussing what Robin Hood did with his looting and what made it okay to steal. As the lead teacher of the class, I was busy getting the class ready for lunch when I overheard this conversation. I did not interfere but sat down with them, listening. I remember the serious manner in which they were conversing; they were very thoughtful, listening and thinking before they answered. I could see how attentive they were in their body language. They waited for each other to conclude their thoughts and then shared their own opinions. There were several "Daddy said" phrases, and those were not random. They relied on those adult opinions to make a point, and they used them thoughtfully.

As a preschool teacher, I had encountered many intriguing conversations between children as young as three years old. Sometimes the topic was a complex ethical question, and sometimes it was wondering what the world is all about. *Where does the moon go? Does it go behind the mountain? How do we know if a tree can hear us?* While I never encountered such thoughtfulness acknowledged in most of the classical developmental theories, in my frequent encounters with young children, this sense of wonderment and deep analysis of what is and what is not prevails.

A friend of mine shared the following about his young grandchildren: "I love when children start to move by themselves. You can look into their eyes and feel their minds churning!" Like my friend, I do love children. I love watching their fingers move and their eyes question whether it is okay to drop a ball and then speculating what my reaction will be if they drop it once, twice, or twenty-two times. I can almost see them thinking, *Will she pick up the ball? What will she say? How will she react?*

As an educator, I love engaging with young children. At one time, young children were considered to have an empty mind or *tabula rasa* that adults could manipulate and form into the person they and society needed. However, modern theories moved away from this idea to acknowledge that children have their own ways of thinking and learning. In education we call these ideas developmental theories. There are theories related to cognitive, moral, and even faith development. However, in many of these theories, young children are still dismissed as dependent and fragile creatures without agency of their own.[1]

This chapter considers an alternative understanding of young children. As I will later explain, I believe that children's minds function on a high level, though differently than adults. The fundamental truth about young children is that they can learn and change, and by doing so, they also change the world around them. A clearer understanding of young children is particularly important for us as we raise children and also as members of churches and faith communities. Our faith practices are built on developmental theories and the resulting assumptions about children and learning.

Before we go any further, let us consider this question:

What Is Childhood?

Alison Gopnik, a psychology professor at University of California–Berkeley, states that childhood is a developmental period of a child's life when they are completely dependent on adults. She asks the obvious question of why human babies need so much care when animal babies can survive on their own in a shorter amount of time. Why do humans need more time to grow? Why are human babies so dependent on adults to care for them? Her answer is that human babies need more time to learn and change. Human babies, unlike other babies, need to learn the accumulation of centuries of knowledge and decades-long survival skills. They need to learn about themselves, their families, and societies, and how to exist in the world. Learning all these skills takes time, so human childhood is extended in comparison with that of animals. Our babies and young children need significantly longer time to change, learn, and grow.[2]

Jean Piaget's Cognitive-Stages Theory and His Methodology

The father of classical cognitive developmental theory is the Swiss psychologist Jean Piaget (1896–1980). Educators refer to his theory to explain how children grow in their mental abilities and learning. According to Piaget, children develop in four distinct stages depending on how their bodies and brains develop and how they can use these abilities to reflect and interact with their environment.

In Piaget's theory, infants and toddlers (birth to age two) do not have the ability to think and reflect. They can drop a ball and watch it fall. Piaget categorizes this as sensory-motor activity and an impulsive activity of an infant learning how to interact with the adults around them. This kind of learning is based on trial and error but is not a thoughtful interaction with the child's surroundings. However, as neuroscience confirms, this activity requires complex cognitive thinking that children can perform—a developmental understanding that emerged after Piaget.[3] I have witnessed many such conversations when children were in contexts such as their home or classroom where loving adults were present who listened to and engaged with them. The new neurological understanding draws an important distinction from what Piaget observed in the young children in his clinical study.

Children and Philosophy

I recall a conversation with my siblings that went something like:

> SIBLING 1: Don't you ever say "why" again!
> SIBLING 2: Why?

Children love asking questions. My younger sister was among them. She had a why for everything, and we, the older sisters, got tired of her questions. However, one person who paid attention to questions like these was the American philosopher Gareth B. Matthews. I was first introduced to Matthews's book *Philosophy and the Young Child* about twenty years ago, and his work continues to linger in my mind. Matthews, a philosopher by training, says that questions children ask are genuinely and intuitively philosophical, and they echo the questions of grand minds in human history. Matthews argues that children are well equipped with the ability to question and wonder. These wonderings parallel philosophical questions that humankind has grappled with since the dawn of time. He advises that caring adults should listen and encourage these questions to nurture wonderment and awe so young children grow in their understanding of the world and of being in the world. Puzzlement and wonder are closely related, Matthews says. Children ask deep questions and do it in a natural way. As Matthews reflects, "That philosophy can begin with a child in so simple a way, says something important about philosophy, and something important about children. It is something that Piaget has missed."[4]

Piaget discarded such imaginative questioning and did not attend to why children stop asking such questions as they grow. Matthews, on the other hand, questions why children stop voicing their philosophical inquiry. If Piaget was correct in his linear developmental theory, then children should ask more of such questions. They may stop asking because questions like "How do I know if I am in a dream?" or "If God is everywhere, then how big is God?" are very often dismissed by adults in children's lives. I think children stop voicing their questions because of social conditioning by the adults who dismiss children's questions, just like Piaget, as foolishness or lacking reasoning.[5]

Piaget also dismissed unusual answers and normalized the repeated answers. In this repetition, Piaget grouped the answers and formed the stages. However, Matthews argues, "But it is the deviant response that is most likely to be philosophically interesting." He further emphasizes that the repeated answer is "an unthinking and un-thought-out product of socialization, whereas the nonconforming response is much more likely to be the fruit of honest reflection."[6]

New Understanding of Young Children

Alison Gopnik not only supports Matthews's idea about children's predisposition to asking philosophical questions but also provides scientific support for these observations. While many scholars treat childhood like a problem to be solved, she argues that "it is what makes all human beings human." Gopnik gives us a new perspective to understand early childhood. "In fact," she says, "psychologists and neuroscientists have discovered that babies not only learn more, but imagine more, care more, and experience more than we would ever have thought possible. In some ways, young children are actually smarter, more imaginative, more caring, and even more conscious than adults."[7]

The key concept for Gopnik and her understanding of early childhood is *change*. What defines humans is their ability to change and create change in the world. Studying children and childhood helps us, the adults, "explain how we change."[8] Some think that humans are bound to their genes, but Gopnik suggests that this view is not comprehensive and does not explain how humans change and develop over time. "The puzzling fact about human beings is that our capacity for change both in our own lives and through history, is the most distinctive and unchanging thing about us."[9]

Learning and change is closely related to what neuroscientists call plasticity. Gopnik defines plasticity as the human ability to change in response to lived experience. Learning and change are neither linear nor unidirectional. As humans change through their lived experiences in the world, they also change the world and imagine new possibilities. "Developing a new theory about the world allows us to imagine other ways the world might be. . . . [Gopnik's] book is about how children develop minds that change the world."[10]

Neuroscience and Young Children

I recall the following conversation from the end of a challenging full-day field trip with one of my three-year-old students.

> ME: Man! You are something!
> CHILD: And I'm way more.

According to Gopnik, neuroscience proves that children's and adults' brains function differently but have "equally complex and powerful minds, brains, and forms of consciousness." This difference in function is to accommodate different requirements in each life stage.[11] To understand these different functions, let us look at how our brains function in different life stages. Neuroscience shows that the neural pathways are more dimly lit in young children's brains than in adult brains. A child's brain map looks like a dimly lighted town while an adult brain looks like a city with bright and fast highways. This is because as a child grows, their brain prunes the pathways that are used less often and reinforces the pathways that are used more frequently. Young brains are incredibly plastic and flexible. This gives them the capacity to change more easily. "But they are much less efficient; they don't work as quickly or effectively" as the grown-up brains do. This is why they need all the time to learn and strengthen the effective neural pathways.[12]

The prefrontal cortex plays a pivotal role in children and adults. This specific part of the brain matures last in humans; however, it plays an important role in development from childhood to maturity. This part of the brain is the "seat of distinctively human abilities. Scientists have located sophisticated capacities for thinking, planning, and control in the prefrontal area."[13] The prefrontal cortex's late development is explained by the same metaphor of dimly lit town images of children's brains and well-lit highways in adults. Development is the process of turning a dimly lit town into a well-lit highway. Gopnik says that this prolonged maturation period enables children to be "super adults," that is, adults who are more able to imagine and learn. This is why children can jump from one topic to another and from one game to another without much difficulty. By doing so, children are open to experiencing the world more freely, as they learn and interact with the world without reservation. Children struggle with focusing, which comes with maturity. The upside of this process is that as a child matures, they are better able to focus. The downside is that the innate gift of being creative and exploring becomes more limited. At this point, the question is not whether children are less capable of focusing or more capable of playful imagining, but rather which characteristic we are valuing: If it is imagination, then children are super adults, and if we are valuing focus and productivity, then adults are better fit to this task.[14]

Simply stated, the prefrontal cortex is very active during early childhood. It keeps developing and changing as the child grows. The development of this part of the brain fundamentally depends on how a child experiences the world. The playful imagination and our learnings as children make us the adults that we are and "provide us with the information that we adults use to plan and control our behavior intelligently."[15]

Children and Religious Education

I recall another conversation with a young child. We were on a long bus ride, and my friend's son, four years old then, wanted to sit with me. He loved talking, and I enjoyed listening to him.

> He asked, "Do you think God is many?"
> I answered him with a question, "What do you mean?"
> After a silent ponder, he said, "I think God should be so big."
> "Why?" I asked.
> "Otherwise, how could God be everywhere?" There was no pondering this time. He had an answer.

Children's ability to ask philosophical questions—to be flexible, to have awe, and to wonder—can also be seen in their ability to ask profound theological questions. *How big is God? Why did God create the moon and stars? Where is heaven?* People of faith of all ages and religious backgrounds ask these questions. It is unfortunate and worrying that children eventually stop asking both philosophical and theological questions as they grow. What should concern us as parents, caregivers, and religious educators is how we can foster continued questioning like this in our children. How can what we heard from Piaget, Gopnik, and Matthews help us in our parenting in faith?

Being aware of Gopnik's research about young children and their ever-active brains is important. Without an understanding of this new research, we might overlook their innate philosophical dispositions and how they could inform us as faith communities in designing children's learning experiences. These theories are important to me because I am concerned about young children's presence at the primary communal acts of our faith: worship. Churches claim to be welcoming and inclusive but exclude young children from worship for just being the active learners they are. For their dimly lit but ever-active prefrontal cortexes and wanting to play and learn by interacting with the world. Often adults in our communities, instead of showing love and acceptance, shun our children from fully participating in their unique childlike ways in the life of worship. This act also discourages their families from attending worship. This exclusion deeply affects the possibilities for young children to learn about their faith. How could they learn how to ask God questions if they do not attend church with the rest of the community of faith?

We know that children need time to learn and that the ability to focus is achieved by practice. Children require time and patience from their parents and caregivers to learn this skill. They also need it from the communities they belong to. Young children are aware of their surroundings, and their brains are active and alert. They know when they are being welcomed and when they are not. Young children are experimenting with the world and learning how to be in it, which is why they cannot sit still as we often demand of them. A welcoming church should be welcoming and hospitable to the young ones who want to learn with them. A welcoming church opens the space for the children to learn by being in worship. A welcoming church models God's love by loving them. Too often churches send children off to an isolated room for the convenience of adults rather than genuinely welcoming them. What Gopnik and Matthews emphasize for us is that children can learn by participating and being with the rest of the church's gathered body. How could the church be more responsive to this challenge?

Guidance for Caregivers and Faith Communities

Knowing about the high-functioning abilities of babies and young children brings us to the most important question: How can we help our young children learn and imagine as they grow to be their wonderful selves that God intended for them to be? How can we reinforce those faithful neurons to light the highways that will take them through their lives of faith and trusting God? To spur our thinking, I offer four suggestions for parents and caregivers as well as congregations.

Make Space to Be and Become

Make the children and their caregivers feel welcomed at the church where the central learning and worship take place. Prioritize this as adults by not sending the children out during the service. Some churches make this happen by replacing a few pews with child-size chairs and toys, allowing the children to play in church. When we do this, we acknowledge that we are a family of faith by respecting children's choices in how to be in the community. It might sound surprising to hear the suggestion that we should respect children's choices. That does not happen very often, but respect is central to raising responsible and thoughtful children. Respect the children for who they are. Welcome and attend to the curious spark and the creativity they bring to our lives. Respect is key to learning and faithfully navigating through life.

Make Space for Questions; Model and Practice Asking Them

Gareth Matthews, author of *Philosophy and the Young Child*, shares that one evening he posed this question to his family: "Is a bicycle a tricycle without one of the wheels?"

The children's task was to come up with similar questions.

> "Is a bicycle a motorbike without a motor?"
> "Is a chair a rocker without runners?"

Matthews calls questions like these "whimsical questions." Whimsical questions are fun and imaginative. They help children to be adventurous and come up with creative questions that challenge the mind and engage the imagination. Whimsical questions could be about any topic, and any of the players can pose the first question. These questions are not about finding answers but rather teaching the art of asking questions by putting the obvious question and logical answer aside. Sometimes coming up with imaginative questions is more engaging and educational than finding a logical answer.[16] We can encourage similar playful questioning by asking God questions. We do not need to be philosophers or theologians to play a questioning game. We just need to listen to the children when they share their thoughts with us. Listening attentively builds relationships between children and adults. This is how the magical sharing of thoughts and questions happens.

Make Space for Not Knowing and Learning

Children have many questions, and their questions might tire us after a long day at work. For situations like this, try to turn the question around and ask your child to share what they think is the answer. In my experience, this opens the door for the child to share more and provides us with a window to their precious inner self.

Once our church was at a retreat in the mountains. I was sitting outdoors with a child and watching the stars.

She asked, "Where did the moon go?"

I answered, "I don't know. Where do you think it has gone?"

After some thinking, she said, "Maybe it fell behind the mountains and. . . ." What followed was a beautiful story about the moon and the woman with a cookie-cutter who lives behind the mountains.

Gopnik states that children know the difference between imaginary and real worlds. However, in imagining new worlds, they shape their own existence in this world. In listening to them, we have the chance to remember those imaginary worlds we used to have in our childhood. Questions children raise bring us back to our faith and our understanding of how our faith shaped our lives in the past and how it might shape our children's and our lives in the future. Our children's questions are the window to our spiritual renewal as we learn to approach faith with humility, living without knowing all the answers, and knowing that God is love and that is enough.

Make Space for Love

Children learn about love very early in their lives. Having loving adults is fundamentally important in children's lives. I believe this is where Piaget missed the most important learning in his study. Children act and behave differently when they are with loving adults whom they know. By observing children only in a clinical setting where they were with persons they did not know, Piaget excluded this important aspect and missed observing children's full potential.

Young children know about love; watch the reaction of children when their caregivers leave them and then return. Even newborns can recognize their mothers and greet them when they enter the room. Strengthening love neurons helps our children grow to become loving adults. Learning about God's love at home or church and experiencing love from caregivers helps children relate to God in more meaningful ways.

One last story . . .

A parent of an almost three-year-old child in my class shared that they were in the car when she started getting nervous about the traffic. Noticing her nervousness, her son interjected from the back seat, "Mommy, breathe!"

She was wondering where her son learned that.

After a short laugh, I admitted that in my preschool class, which included her son, we practice breathing to help us center when we feel anxious and upset.

This incident illustrates that young children can connect the daily practices learned at daycare with their parent or caregiver's experiences. This child remembered a practice that calmed them down and transferred the learning to a similar anxiety-producing situation. How could this happen if children were not capable of such complex mental processes as the classical developmental theories assume? Next time a child drops a ball and you catch it, think: Is this a tedious movement as Piaget thought it was? Is this a child's way of connecting with you, and your positive response is reinforcing their love neurons as Gopnik would suggest? Or as Matthews says, is the child learning about where the ball goes when it is not in their hand?

When I play games with children, I think that a game is a child's way of teaching me about their world. When I respond to their invitation, I teach them to trust the world. They are opening their inner world to me, and I am welcoming them into mine. I see God at the center of this relationship. I see how I learned about God and, by welcoming them in worship, I am teaching them that a welcoming God is at the center of our community of faith. I am strengthening faithful neurons of well-lit highways and hopefully nurturing some questioning and imaginative curiosity toward being in the world.

Questions for Discussion

1. Wasoian gives four suggestions for how parents and caregivers can help children "grow to be their wonderful selves that God intended for them to be." Which of those suggestions resonates with you? Why? How do you live out what Wasoian suggests?
2. When have children taught you? What did you learn?
3. What do you need to do to be open to the insights and knowledge of children? What helps children to be open to sharing their insights?

Notes

1. An example of this is Piaget's cognitive stages theory.
2. Alison Gopnik, *The Philosophical Baby: What Children's Minds Tell Us About Truth, Love, and Meaning of Life* (New York: Picador, 2009), 10.
3. Piaget's stages are: (1) Sensor/motor (birth to two years). Infant gradually becomes able to organize activities in relation to the environment through sensory and motor activities. (2) Preoperational (two to seven years). Child develops a representational system and uses symbols to represent people, places, and events. Language and imaginative play are important manifestations of this stage. Thinking is still not logical. (3) Concrete operations (seven to eleven years). Child can solve problems logically if they are focused on the here and now but cannot think abstractly. (4) Formal operations (eleven years through adulthood). Person can think abstractly, deal with hypothetical situations, and think about possibilities. Cited in Diane E. Papalia et al., *Human Development* (New York: McGraw-Hill, 2004), 32.
4. Gareth B. Matthews, *Philosophy and the Young Child* (Cambridge, MA: Harvard University Press, 1980), vii, 2, 55.
5. Matthews, *Philosophy and the Young Child*, 38.
6. Matthews, *Philosophy and the Young Child*, 38.
7. Gopnik, *The Philosophical Baby*, 4–8.
8. Gopnik, *The Philosophical Baby*, 6.
9. Gopnik, *The Philosophical Baby*, 7.
10. Gopnik, *The Philosophical Baby*, 8.
11. Gopnik, *The Philosophical Baby*, 9–10.
12. Gopnik, *The Philosophical Baby*, 11–12.
13. Gopnik, *The Philosophical Baby*, 12.
14. Gopnik, *The Philosophical Baby*, 13.
15. Gopnik, *The Philosophical Baby*, 13–14.
16. Matthews, *Philosophy and the Young Child*, 76–77.

References

Gopnik, Alison. *The Philosophical Baby: What Children's Minds Tell Us About Truth, Love, and the Meaning of Life*. New York: Picador, 2009.

Matthews, Gareth B. *Philosophy and the Young Child*. Cambridge, MA: Harvard University Press, 1980.

Papalia, Diane E., Sally Wendkos Olds, and Ruth Duskin Feldman. *Human Development*. New York: McGraw-Hill, 2004.

Section 11
The Sticky Stuff: Caregiver Practices in Times of Challenge

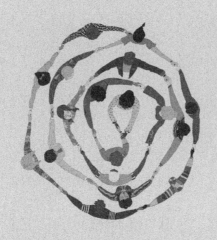

6

Nurturing Faith through Intergenerational Storytelling and Play

G. LEE RAMSEY JR. AND MARY LESLIE DAWSON-RAMSEY

The assault of COVID-19 from February 2020 into 2022 forced religious congregations to modify almost every aspect of communal life. Faith leaders had to adapt weekly worship and preaching, religious education and formation, administration, fellowship, and pastoral care to this terrifying existential threat. Some congregations met the challenge with creativity and courage. Others became dormant, overwhelmed by fear and indecision. Within the United Methodist Church, our denominational home, COVID-19 induced fear mixed with the angst caused by the denomination-wide struggle over the place of LGBTQIA+ persons within the church. Divisions widened. At the local level, the splintering of congregational life mirrored the denominational division at the global level. Within this context, what was and is possible for faith formation, especially with our children and youth?

Our own small, rural congregation in West Tennessee of approximately forty active households (mostly extended families with generational ties to the church) thrashed around, wondering what ministries were possible and safe to strengthen community life and nurture faith. How could we nurture the children and youth? How could we resource parents and other caregivers in the home? How could we hold the congregation together in hope when despair threatened the days ahead? With limited resources, including less-than-adequate internet speeds, what sorts of weekly and episodic worship, educational, and community ministries were even feasible?

Responding to these challenges, our congregation imagined and implemented several intergenerational activities that were designed to nurture faith and community formation of children, youth, and adults focused on the big stories of the Christian tradition: Easter, Christmas, and Pentecost. Here we describe these congregation-wide events that took place over eighteen to twenty-four months at the height of the COVID-19 pandemic as both *play* and *story*.[1] They were intentional efforts to invite creative, playful, intergenerational participation in community and faith formation around key chapters within the Christian story, especially in a time of protracted crisis. Following these descriptions, we offer brief interpretations of how similar intergenerational story-themed and playful events may be helpful in the work of Christian formation of children, youth, and adults in more ordinary times.

Nurturing the Hope of Easter

Easter fell on April 12, 2020, exactly one full month after the first official lockdown began across the United States and within our own community in West Tennessee. The contagion was spreading unchecked. Thousands succumbed to death across the globe; fear pervaded. Our church, like most others in the area, closed its doors to weekly worship and education to protect public health. Yet Easter was upon us, the day of all days that trumpets the hope of the resurrected Christ, who triumphs over fear and death. But that was exactly what we were experiencing all around and within us: fear and death. We would hold no in-person Easter sunrise service, no community breakfast, no egg hunt for the band of children and youth that had brightened every Easter in the past. How could we, then, enflesh the hope of the gospel within the fearful community of faith?

Through phone calls, texts, and emails, several of the church leaders and Sunday school teachers developed a plan. They assembled packets of craft materials to distribute to every church family with children and/or youth. The packet contained supplies and simple instructions for making colorful butterflies using clothespins, fabric, and markers. They invited the children and youth (with the help of the adults in their lives) to make several of these butterflies. They would not only keep the butterflies for themselves but place them in the mailboxes of other church members, particularly the elderly, homebound, and members who lived in care facilities. The simple Scripture-based verse—"Christ is risen"—was attached to each butterfly (see Matthew 28:5-7 and Luke 24:5-7). Then parents, caregivers, and grandparents drove their kids throughout the community, placing simple signs of Easter hope in mailboxes and on the doorsteps of other church members and friends. One family drove more than thirty-five miles to place a butterfly on our car's windshield!

Additionally, one traditional highlight of this congregation for Easter Sunday morning is decorating a large outdoor cross with spring flowers. Normally we do this within the Easter sunrise service as an affirmation of faith in response to the good news. While the planning team decided it would not be safe to carry out this ritual corporately, we invited everyone in the congregation to bring their own flowers throughout the Easter weekend to adorn the cross. And while they were at the church, we provided tulips, daffodils, and lilies that church members, if they wanted, could plant in the church garden. Several parents and grandparents joined their children in planting these spring flowers.

The Zoom-mediated sermon (with text version available) for Easter Sunday from Matthew 28:1-10 emphasized living with hope in the midst of fear. In that passage, the two Marys find the tomb empty. They rush with fear yet joy right into the presence of the resurrected Christ, who tells them what all of us needed to hear on Easter Sunday 2020: "Do not be afraid" (Matthew 28:5). Joy stands before us even amid fear. The sermon declared the intergenerational butterfly making and delivery as signs of hope for the whole community. The church and culture were locked down, but Christ is our living hope, showing us how to be the church under duress—how to actively celebrate life over death.

Children, youth, and adults of all ages participated in the making and sharing of these Easter symbols. They did so under the pall of COVID-19, an experience of communal suffering and death, yet the butterflies and flowers pointed toward the new dawn of Easter. The phone calls rolled out, the text messages pinged, families sent in their Easter photos to be posted on Facebook for all to see, and many brought flowers to the cross. No, it was not corporate worship and faith formation in the usual way that our congregation cherished on Easter. But this set of adaptive Easter rituals helped knit the congregation together in hope at the beginning of the pandemic and gave us some confidence that the church could create ways to continue nurturing the faith of people of all ages under extraordinarily adverse circumstances. We adapted and found new ways to tell the story using the gifts and offerings of the congregation.

Playfully Sharing the Christmas Story

By the time Advent and Christmas rolled around in 2020, we had been able to worship outdoors for a couple of months in the early fall, but a nationwide spike in COVID cases and the arrival of cold weather once again prohibited safe corporate worship. We reluctantly returned to Zoom worship in early November. Attendance at Zoom worship throughout COVID was small but important for those who participated and for those who did not participate but knew that the church was gathering, even in a virtual way. We were despondent that we would not be able to gather in person for the beloved Advent and Christmas season.

The planning team went back into action. This time we called on the woodworkers, those with jigsaws, bandsaws, and scroll saws. And we called for the arts and crafts talents of an even larger swath of the multigenerational congregation than we had at Easter. The activity was to design, cut, and decorate fifty crèches, complete with a stable, star, sheep, shepherds, camels, magi, Mary, Joseph, and the baby Jesus in the manger. Imagine how one of the grandfathers of the church reacted when asked to cut fifty ready-to-assemble wooden stables from a template, and another great-grandparent couple was asked to cut out all the figures that would inhabit and surround the stable. But after some good-natured grumbling, these retired church members put their hearts and hands into preparing fifty stables and a whole host of nativity characters.

Here the playfulness of this formation event around the Christmas story came to the forefront. Once the woodworking was complete, the planning team assembled kits with paint pens, cloth, glue, and glitter, along with an explanation sheet inviting all who were interested to help decorate the crèche and characters in preparation for the celebration of Jesus' birth. For example, one family would decorate ten sheep and ten Marys while another family would decorate five magi riding on camels and five shepherds. The idea was to engage as many households as possible in this intergenerational event and then to assemble a crèche for each household in the church. Some of the wise men arrived at the stable wearing intricately designed miniature robes and crowns. Some of the sheep were simply made with cotton balls and noses colored with black felt tip markers. The diversity of decorations was stunning. It is difficult to describe how much playful, joyous energy this event created within the congregation as we sought a fresh way for the whole congregation to participate in the Christmas story even if not together in the sanctuary.

On the targeted weekend before Christmas, members delivered their decorated holy families, sheep, and camels to the church fellowship hall, where a small team of crèche builders assembled all the pieces to make fifty nativity sets. Each piece of the collectively made crèches was signed by the church member who decorated it. On the bottom of each stable, a team member wrote: "Created by church members December 2020, during the COVID-19 pandemic." During the week leading up to Christmas, each church family came to the sanctuary to retrieve their nativity set. No two were alike, but each one bore the playful creativity of several other church members. Each one reminds us of the incarnation of God in the baby Jesus, born in trying circumstances, amid social and political oppression, into a world marred by human frailty and divided by human sin.

No, in the year of our Lord 2020, the church wasn't able to congregate to worship the newborn baby Jesus. We were not able to sing together the beloved Christmas hymns. We were not able to enact our own rendition of the Christmas pageant with lost sheep wandering through the pews and angels belting out "Glory to God in the highest" while precariously perched on rickety stepladders. We grieved much. But we found something else. Children, youth, parents, caregivers, grandparents, aunts, and uncles all had a hand in sharing the Christmas story through a congregation-wide creative event. To the best of our ability, no household was left out. Members delivered Christmas crèches to those who were homebound or unable to participate in the meaning-making event.

The Christmas story was already given in the early chapters of Matthew and Luke, but we found a way under trying conditions to make the story uniquely our own. We would be willing to bet that if church members remember anything about how the church carried on during COVID-19, this intergenerational, congregation-wide event would be high on the list. As Tanya Marie Eustace Campen reminds us, "When families gather to read, share, watch or experience a story together, we enter a holy moment of wonder and discovery, a moment to which we come with curiosity, and wonder."[2] Indeed, it was gratifying at Christmas the next year for us to see, while visiting a ninety-two-year-old widowed member of the congregation, that he had placed the handmade crèche on his coffee table to help him celebrate Christ's birth.

Re-membering the Congregation at Pentecost

With vaccines widely available, the church and culture began to emerge from the pandemic swamp in 2022. One final action was needed to complete the cycle of birth, death, resurrection, and new life within the body of Christ: a celebration of Pentecost. Normally, Pentecost worship involves some form of children and youth waving cut-out tongues of flame or incorporating several languages and cultural traditions in the liturgy and worship. But this particular Sunday would be the Sunday of re-membering the church on its official birthday. Coming out of the long winter of COVID-19, the church could finally come back together for worship, fellowship, and formation. But how could we make this regathering significant and tied to the larger story of the church? How would we symbolize the broken body of Christ joined together in faith, discipleship, and witness, especially when division in church and culture still threatened and fear for personal and public health was still palpable?

The planning team for nurture and worship came together one last time. They conceived and outlined a tree with a single trunk and many branches on a large sheet of plywood. Then one of the men of the church cut the entire plywood tree into multiple squares. Imagine a wood tabletop cut into four-inch squares. The team members then distributed one square per church household, inviting each household to paint and decorate their square according to the prescribed sketch and color scheme (brown for the tree trunk, blue for the sky, green for the leaves, red for apples on the tree, etc.). Only the planning team members knew what the puzzle was in its entirety.

On the day of our first reunited worship service, our act of affirmation was the assembling of all the pieces of the tree. Children, youth, and adults brought their pieces forward to create the now freshly painted tree, a symbol of the newly united church (scriptural echoes of "I am the vine; you are the branches" [John 15:5; see verses 1–8]; one body, many members [1 Corinthians 12:12-27]; and the tree of life [Revelation 2:7, 22:1-21]. Supporting this symbolic act, the sermon proclaimed the gift of new life and unity amid diversity and difference, even the political and social divisions present in our congregation. We are one body with many gifts yet one Spirit that unites us all (1 Corinthians 12).

Following the benediction, the congregation gathered outside the church on the edge of a large field that bordered the church property. There, as prearranged, a person from the neighboring county had brought three white homing doves. After prayer and another word about the Spirit's power in the form of a dove to unite the church and gather us home, the birds were released into the open sky. They circled the church several times and then headed off into the distance to return to their own home.

In this rural congregation on the day of Pentecost, when we first gathered corporately at the end of the worst of COVID-19, the natural image of the church as a deeply rooted family tree made sense. When we concluded the worship service by singing "I Am the Church," with all ages lifting their voices together, and when we watched those doves high in the sky circling our place of worship and faith formation, it was clear that we had thus far weathered together a huge cultural, congregational, and ongoing denominational crisis. Although we had some losses along the way, we remained united in worship, nurture, and witness. "So we, who are many, are one body in Christ" (Romans 12:5).

Story, Play, and Christian Nurture: Conclusions

The church has always found ways to proclaim, teach, enact, and pass on the central mysteries of the faith asserted in the liturgy of Holy Communion: "Christ has died; Christ is risen; Christ will come again." In the third decade of the twenty-first century, in the wake of a global pandemic, church and cultural divisions, and a human-made environmental catastrophe, the church is clearly changing and reshaping how we gather, how we serve, and how we form the faith of upcoming generations. As many Christian educators are pointing out, there is no one right way of Christian formation. There is no one key but a whole set of keys worth trying to keep the doors open where faith can flow across generations. The answer to John Westerhoff's apt question, "Will our children have faith?" is clearly "Yes."[3] The issue is what kind of faith in content and practice. Who will nurture the faiths of today and tomorrow? And how will such faith formation be carried out?

We hope that faithful caregivers can find some direction by turning to intergenerational practices of faith formation that include large amounts of play and storytelling. Here we have done little more than show how essential stories within the larger Christian tradition can be creatively embraced by all ages outside of the arena of the traditional Sunday school class and sanctuary. We are fully aware that others have already pointed the way to reimagine Sunday school beyond 9:45 on Sunday mornings, a movement within Christian education that was put to the test by COVID-19. The imaginative and creative work of children and youth Sunday school teachers, and the traditional age-based Sunday school classroom can be reimagined for the home and the whole church, and hopefully not just in response to a global pandemic. We can invite adults and caregivers of all ages to play with children and youth as together they retell the stories of faith, whether by cocreating clothespin butterflies (Easter), hand-painted nativity scenes (Christmas), and puzzle-designed symbols of the church, or by holding hands while watching doves arch through the sky (Pentecost). Somehow, playing together around symbol-making and storytelling activities helps us all realize that child's play is faithful and life-giving.

In the decades ahead, some adults and children may find their spiritual homes remain moored to the institutional church, while others may find the church as a necessary but supplemental resource to other primary spiritual communities (family, friends, coworkers, creative collectives, activist organizations, etc.).[4] Whatever forms the faith of the next generations embraces and whatever their stance in relationship to the church of previous generations, communal belonging will always be critical, created as we are by God for one another. But it is not just belonging that matters. For those who most closely identify with the Christian story, it is belonging to an intergenerational body of storytellers who find self, others, and calling in the playfully serious affirmation that "Christ has died; Christ is risen; Christ will come again."

Questions for Discussion

1. What are the strengths found in intergenerational ministry, particularly in worship settings?
2. How do we incorporate play into the life of our church?
3. What are the ways we galvanize people for action? How can these strategies be used regardless of whether there is a crisis?

Notes

1. This article is primarily descriptive of several imaginative attempts to nurture Christian formation during the COVID-19 lockdowns. We do offer brief interpretation along the way and in the conclusion, but our primary aim is to describe one United Methodist congregation's efforts to playfully attend to the Christian story in a time of church and cultural distress. The authors were both involved with the leadership of the congregation and of these formational events but view themselves as part of the nurture and education team comprised of several gifted and faithful

laity. For a concise, professional summary of descriptive, interpretive, and imaginative approaches to Christian formation, see Karen-Marie Yust, "Whose Children Are They? Talking about Responsibility for Children's Religious Education," *Religious Education* 118, no. 2 (2023): 87–93, https://doi.org/10.1080/00344087.2023.2198819. For a helpful discussion of religious formation as play and story, among the many, see Jerome W. Berryman (2023), "Wondering about Whose Children They Are," *Religious Education* 118, no. 2, (2023): 94–96, https://doi.org/10.1080/00344087.2023.2184022; and Tanya Marie Eustace Campden, *Holy Work with Children: Making Meaning Together* (Eugene, OR: Pickwick, 2021). For a comprehensive approach to intergenerational faith formation, see John Roberto, *Lifelong Faith: Formation for All Ages and Generations* (New York: Church Publishing, 2022).

2. Tanya Marie Eustace Campen, "Holy Work with Families: Living Out Our Faith Together," in *Let the Children Lead: Exploring Children's Spirituality Today*, ed. Elizabeth DeGaynor (Alexandria, VA: VTS Press, 2023), 67.

3. John H. Westerhoff III, *Will Our Children Have Faith?*, 3rd rev. ed. (New York: Morehouse, 2012).

4. See the suggestive comment by Yust, "Whose Children Are They?", 92.

7

The Spirituality of Grand*parenting: When Grandparents Become Primary Caregivers

TERESA E. JEFFERSON-SNORTON

Introduction

The phenomenon of grandparents becoming the primary caregivers in the lives of American children is expanding at significant rates. Historically, when extended families were geographically located in a small radius, grandparents played a key role in the lives of their grandchildren. However, that pattern shifted as relocation to cities took younger families with children farther away from grandparents, aunts, uncles, and cousins. Within African American communities (and other communities of color), the Great Migration from the South to the North that began in the 1910s resulted in countless children being left with grandparents as their parents moved to seek employment in northern factories and businesses.

I grew up with both sets of grandparents within a few miles, and their influence on my life is undeniable. But they were not my primary caregivers. However, in 2005 my own life was altered when I became primary caregiver to my newborn grandson. During that time, I became keenly aware of internal changes in my spirit, in addition to the external changes in how I arranged my life and used my time.

Internally my sense of identity shifted, as did my sense of time and purpose. Prayers and conversations with God in the form of questions emerged. This chapter is an effort to provide some insight into the internal process that occurs when grandparents become the primary parents. The title of this chapter is intended to convey that shift by identifying this process as grand*parenting. The asterisk accompanying the word *grand* is used to describe something that is the largest or most important item of its kind. "Grand*parenting" conveys the idea that when grandparents become primary caregivers, parenting becomes the primary task in daily life. This shift occurs at a time in life when most assumed their parenting days were over and life would revolve around events and activities related to those in their mature years of life (retirement, downsizing, travel, etc.).

The need for a deeper understanding of the needs of grand*parenting within congregations is becoming more evident as this phenomenon becomes more common. Journalist A. J. Baime writes, "U.S. census data (2020) shows that 7.1 million American grandparents are living with their grandchildren under 18. Some 2.3 million of those grandparents are responsible for their grandchildren. About a third of grandchildren living with grandparents who are responsible for them are younger than 6. About half of the grandparents who are responsible for their grandchildren are 60 and over, according to census data."[1]

The challenges of grand*parenting are reflected in other realities. According to a blog titled "The Most Surprising Grandparents Raising Grandchildren Statistics and Trends in 2023," disabled grandparents make up 15 percent of those providing care, 21 percent have incomes below the poverty level, and 39 percent have been primary parenting for at least five years.[2] It would seem appropriate to label grand*parenting as a life-changing event that not only alters one's identity, focus, time, and resources, but also their faith and spirituality and how it is utilized to cope with the radical changes in lifestyle and responsibilities.

Grand*parents must be encouraged to use their faith for their own grounding and growth as they also use it to help in the development and faith formation of their grandchildren. Too often, overwhelmed with new responsibilities, grand*parents may find it easier to withdraw from congregational life to have more time for the grandchildren or to avoid the disruptions that may occur when these additional duties are assumed. Congregations should be intentional in acknowledging the unique life of grand*parents, the shift in priorities in their lives, and the increased needs that grand*parents have for inclusion and support.

Congregations can help by making programmatic and schedule changes to accommodate grand*parents. Grand*parents may struggle with time management, especially if they are still working. Empty nesters and those who are retired often have free time to pursue interests and activities of their choice. Once grandchildren become a primary responsibility, time becomes a valuable and limited commodity. The time available and the time of day and week available for religious and church activities may suddenly shift. Evening meetings can be a challenge for those with school-aged grandchildren. Weekends may become filled with sports and other youth activities. Focused participation in worship with children in tow (especially preschool-aged) becomes more difficult if the service does not capture the interest of children or if no children's church alternative is available.

Equally important to scheduling is the need to assist grand*parents in understanding and articulating the spiritual impact of their new role. These conversations are categorically different from those that typically occur within the "senior ministry" in local congregations. Often we identify our spirituality by the religious events and activities we participate in, such as attending worship, serving in various capacities, doing outreach, and so on. However, the need to have a deeper understanding of one's own spirituality to share it with others is critical for all believers—parents and grand*parents as well. Spirituality goes beyond events and activities, religious rituals and practices, and even doctrine and polity. Our spirituality is grounded in how our faith shapes our interpretation of the world, our lives, and others through a theological lens. For Christians, the theological lens is that of belief in one God, whom we understand as Parent, Child, and Spirit (or historically as Father, Son, and Holy Spirit). There are several formal and technical definitions of spirituality, but I find the descriptions in "Milton Hay's Four Dimensions of Spirituality" below especially helpful in unpacking the concept of spirituality.[3]

Milton Hay's Four Dimensions of Spirituality

RELIGIOUS NEEDS are what shapes one's search for meaning. Subscription to or rejection of different religious philosophies alters one's approach to the search for meaning and can shape the resulting conclusions. Also, certain religious rites and rituals can be used as means of expressing spirituality.

COMMUNITY is the human environment in which spiritual development occurs. One's spiritual community can include, but is not limited to, one's family, friends, church or other religious organization, coworkers, or classmates. The community dimension, like the other three dimensions of spirituality, is, by its nature, highly personal and individualized.

MEANING fosters spiritual development through its exploration. Spirituality develops within the context of a search for answers about and meaning in life, death, pain, nature, love, or any number of other seemingly inexplicable concepts or experiences. Often, through the spirituality developed in the search for meaning, one may achieve a certain peace with existence that lessens the importance of intellectual answers to the aforementioned difficult concepts.

INNER RESOURCES are the senses, emotions, and personal abilities that one must access and strengthen in order to enhance one's chances of transcending difficulties through spirituality in order to fully participate in the spiritual act of living. Inner resources may be evoked out through such activities as prayer, yoga, meditation, reflection, lovemaking, exercise, singing, and laughter.

While Hay's definitions of the various dimensions of spirituality are helpful, my articulation of these dimensions is slightly different and has evolved out of prior knowledge and personal experience. For grand*parents, I see a more targeted specificity of these four dimensions as essential:

- Religious needs: an awareness of the transcendent
- Community: a sense of belonging
- Meaning: a sense of meaning
- Inner resources: a means of creativity

Like Hay's categories, these four provide a backdrop for examining how the spirituality of grand*parenting requires targeted attention. While every individual has these same spiritual needs, the shifts grand*parents experience must be noted as a part of their personal life and faith journey.

An Awareness of the Transcendent

Like almost all grand*parents, I became a grand*parent quite unexpectedly and under less-than-ideal circumstances. My son had completed one year of college when he informed me that his girlfriend was pregnant. Once I was past the initial shock and anger, I began to wonder why God had allowed this to happen. I raised my children properly in the church. I had taught my son the realities and practicalities of human sexuality and reproduction. Other grand*parents may have similar musings when their children have babies without the benefit of marriage or become unable to parent due to under- or unemployment, addictions, mental health issues, incarceration, or other circumstances. We raise our children to be the best, so it can be shocking and disappointing when their lives are disrupted by situations beyond their immediate control or by poor decisions that also involve or impact children.

Our spirituality as Christians hinges on our belief in God as a transcendent being. God's presence in our lives gives us a sense of safety and security that extends beyond rational or logical understanding. An awareness of transcendent knowledge and power that surpasses our human limitations provides a source of comfort in challenging and troubling times. Our spirituality grounds us in believing beyond what we see, maintaining hope and living in anticipation of a better future.

When I became a grand*parent, I found myself wondering about God's plan for my life because, in my mind, this was not how I had envisioned welcoming the next generation. My grandson was premature, barely considered viable at twenty-seven weeks in utero. Weighing in at only one pound, fourteen ounces, he spent his first eight weeks in the hospital hooked to machines and fed intravenously. He was not expected to survive. His college-aged parents lacked the emotional maturity and the physical resources to properly care for him. When he was discharged from the hospital, they picked him up, brought him and his heart monitor to my house, dropped him off, and left with some excuse about an errand. They were completely overwhelmed, and as his care demanded more and more attention, it became quite evident that they could not take care of this child. I became a grand*parent indeed.

Grand*parenting may disrupt dreams and plans that were felt to be in accord with God's will and plan for our lives. We are challenged to integrate this new development into an assumed or planned life narrative. Research suggests that many parents (and grand*parents) have a "fragmented spirituality" primarily focused on personal salvation. This narrow, one-dimensional view of a relationship to the transcendent renders many people ill-equipped to deal with the complexities of today's world and the daily world of their children. Grand*parents need to be assisted in cultivating an "integrating spirituality" when the unanticipated primary responsibility for child-rearing becomes a part of their reality. Almeda Wright posits that an "integrating spirituality" addresses the dissonance in one's inner and outer world in order to cultivate congruence of mind, body, and spirit.[4] The relationship to the transcendent, thus, is not just for personal salvation but for individual, communal, and systemic transformation. Grand*parents can easily become focused on "Why is God letting this happen to me/my family?" at the expense of seeing how this new role calls them to another level of spiritual growth and transformation that could benefit them individually and others communally and systemically.

A Sense of Belonging

Hay cites community as an essential dimension of spirituality. One's definition of community is highly personal, individualized, and often unarticulated. Having a place to belong, as well as a group of people one would consider their inner circle or support system is critical to well-being, both spiritually and physically. Becoming a grand*parent may also disrupt this formed community, as roles and responsibilities change. While the local church where I worshiped was sensitive to and equipped for the presence of children, the activities in which I typically ministered did not have to consider the presence of children when we met. Most of the pastoral leadership had adult children, so they (we) came to meetings and activities without children in tow. It was initially awkward for me as I arrived with a baby carrier in hand, and my attention was divided between what was happening and the needs of my infant grandson.

My circle of friends included many grandparents but noncustodial. Our lunches and get-togethers became difficult for me with a newborn and later a toddler. In addition, because of his health needs, I frequently was in the company of young mothers at doctor's appointments, physical therapy, preschool events, and other activities related to my grandson's care. It was difficult to relate to them beyond conversations about the children's needs because I was twenty to thirty years older and often found my responses to be more "mothering" than as a peer. With all these shifts, I was keenly aware that I had lost my sense of belonging due to grand*parenting.

Grand*parenting requires a sensitivity to the changing roles and responsibilities related to primary parenting. Even within families these changes are often not recognized and acknowledged, and family members continue to maintain their original expectations for the grand*parents. Other grandparents or same-generation friends may be unable to relate to the concerns of grand*parents.

Finding, cultivating, and maintaining a sense of community and belonging can be challenging for grand*parents. The Christian faith is built around the concept of community—the congregation, the ecclesia, the assembly. When grand*parenting interrupts the usual opportunities for participating in this vital faith community, the ability to maintain a healthy spirituality may be compromised. While congregations often work to make sure they are "child-friendly," trends suggest that they also should consider how to be friendly places for grand*parents. In addition to adjusting schedules, local congregations can support this unique demographic through support groups and activities for grand*parents both with and without their grandchildren.

A Sense of Meaning

In his seminal work "A Theory of Human Motivation" Abraham Maslow placed physiological and social needs at the base of the hierarchy of needs. As basic needs are met, individuals are able to focus on "esteem" needs. Beyond the basic "esteem" needs for status and recognition are the needs for competence, mastery, and self-confidence.[5] These characteristics and the opportunity to pursue them give individuals a sense of meaning. Viktor Frankl identified having a purpose that one feels positive about as key to survival. When it comes to spirituality, purpose is vital in having a sense of meaning in one's life and thriving. Frankl continued, describing a psychotherapeutic method to help people discover and live their purpose: the completion of tasks, caring for another person, or finding meaning by facing suffering with dignity.[6] In my own experience, the newly acquired task of grand*parenting provided and perhaps even bolstered my sense of meaning and purpose.

I became a grand*parent at the age of fifty. My vocation, career, and ministry were humming along quite well. I had mastered the tasks of my professional work. I felt confident and competent. My young adult sons were heavily engaged in their own life and daily activities. I was thinking about what it would be like to be an empty nester, especially since I was a single parent for almost a decade and a half. My grandchild's entrance into my life was not only a generational marker and significant life transition but an event that redirected my attention to a meaningful, relevant task (parenting, nurturing, and caregiving of the young) that I had virtually dismissed from my musings about the future.

Although grand*parenting can be daunting and overwhelming, it can also be a time of revival and newfound purpose and meaning. People who empathize with the burden grand*parents experience are often surprised when those caregivers do not feel burdened, as was in my case. On the other hand, some grand*parents become so aware of their lack of capacity for parenting at this stage in life that they struggle to find a positive sense of purpose and meaning in the experience. Congregations and faith communities can be safe places for both kinds of grand*parents as they rediscover or wrestle with finding meaning. Providing time space for intentional conversations and acceptance of different perspectives on the grand*parenting journey can provide support and affirmation. Similar to the ways in which new parents find ways to support one another, opportunities promoted by the local congregation can aid grand*parents in creating networks of support and sharing of resources. Consider events for exchanging childcare, clothing, tutoring, information about activities, and so on.

A Means of Creativity

Further up Maslow's hierarchy of needs are cognitive needs, including the need for creativity, foresight, curiosity, and knowledge. Accompanying our need for meaning is the need to feel that we are making unique contributions to the family, community, or world. This means of creativity is a form of giving back as well as legacy building—that by which one will be remembered.

Research reveals that repetitive tasks or work performed without a sense of meaning and purpose can quickly lead to stress, boredom, depression, and burnout. The ability to contribute to the design, implementation, and result of our work (creativity) leads to a greater sense of autonomy and agency.[7] This explains why people can find joy in tasks that others assume to be work, like cooking and cleaning. The ability to craft one's own approach to a given activity supports a sense of inner strength and possibility.

I found great value in being in a context that required me to keep up with the latest trends, watch the new cartoons and children's movies, read the current versions of children's books, learn about their music, activities, and above all, technology. Grand*parenting helped me not to become stuck in my old and familiar ways of being.

This dimension of spirituality offers many opportunities for grand*parents as individuals and as a part of the faith community. Very little has been written about the experience of grand*parents, and these stories must be captured. Grand*parents actively create new rituals and practices that make sense for the generations that live under one roof. This family model goes beyond what we have previously known about nuclear, extended, and blended families. This new knowledge should shape our family and children's ministries.

Many grand*parents walk the delicate balance of functioning as primary parents while helping their grandchildren maintain some connection to their biological parent(s). The creativity required to do so in a healthy manner can teach all of us how to cultivate wholeness amid brokenness. When my grandson celebrated birthdays, we took many pictures. A favorite after-party activity was to sit together to create a picture album to share with his mother later, since she had moved to another town. Taking the time to do this helped my grandson stay connected to an absent parent and forced me to think intentionally and creatively about maintaining this connection. Grand*parenting is a prime opportunity to re-create the concepts of what it means to be "family."

Conclusion

The phenomenon of grand*parenting is likely one that will continue and grow. Faith communities, pastors, and others who want to ensure faith development throughout the life cycle must develop an understanding of this new family model. Even when grand*parents have a significant and strong faith, the new experience of becoming primary parents again can challenge identity, energy, meaning, and purpose. It can challenge and change one's relationship with God, as well as the relationship with the congregation and even one's own family.

Grand*parenting draws our attention back to a classic but revised definition of extended family and multigenerational households. The re-creating and revising of roles and rituals becomes front and center in the home. Challenge and opportunity reside side by side in the grand*parenting home. The faith community can and should be a part of reconciling and resolving the pain, frustration, and shifts that are inherently part of this life-changing experience.

Grand*parents are a group that needs to be seen, heard, and supported as they offer love and nurture to the children of their children, often an unexpected role that evolves because of painful, traumatic, or unexpected circumstances. For grand*parents to be up to the task, they must attend to their own spirituality. Blessed are those who have a community of faith to support them as well.

Questions for Discussion

1. How do we in the faith community form grand*parent support groups in an intergenerational way?

2. How do we support parents and caregivers who might be parenting in nontraditional roles?
3. What opportunities are there to support and bear witness to responses of shock or grief at how we became caregivers?
4. How can we support children who are being parented in nontraditional ways?

Notes

1. A. J. Baime, "When Grandparents Are Called to Parent—Again," *AARP*, March 2, 2023, https://www.aarp.org/home-family/friends-family/info-2023/grandparents-become-parents-again.html#:~:text=Grandfamily%20Resources&text=U.S.%20census%20data%20shows%20that,them%20are%20younger%20than%206.

2. "The Most Surprising Grandparents Raising Grandchildren Statistics and Trends in 2023," accessed August 28, 2023, https://blog.gitnux.com/grandparents-raising-grandchildren-statistics/.

3. "Milton Hay's Four Dimensions of Spirituality," accessed August 20, 2023, http://www.math.brown.edu/tbanchof/Yale/project13/dimensions.htm.

4. The terms "fragmented spirituality" and "integrated spirituality" were employed as descriptors in *Religious Parenting: Transmitting Faith and Values in Contemporary America*, Christian Smith, Bridget Ritz, and Michael Rotolo (Princeton, NJ: Princeton University Press, 2020); and in Almeda M. Wright, *The Spiritual Lives of Young African Americans* (New York: Oxford University Press, 2017).

5. Abraham Maslow, "A Theory of Human Motivation," *Psychological Review* 50, no. 4 (1943): 270–396.

6. Viktor Frankl, *Man's Search for Meaning* (1946; repr., Boston: Beacon, 2006).

7. Jennifer Moss, *The Burnout Epidemic: The Rise of Chronic Stress and How We Can Fix It* (Brighton, MA: Harvard Business Review Press, 2021).

8

Fostering Resilient Children: Insights from a Freirean Approach

DÉBORA B. AGRA JUNKER

Education is the point at which we decide whether we love the world enough to assume responsibility for it and by the same token save it from that ruin which, except for renewal, except for the coming of the new and young, would be inevitable. And education, too, is where we decide whether we love our children enough not to expel them from our world and leave them to their own devices, nor to strike from their hands their chance of undertaking something new, something unforeseen by us, but to prepare them in advance for the task of renewing a common world.[1]

In recent years, we have faced challenges that have reshaped the global landscape, notably the intensification of social, racial, and political conflicts around the world, as well as environmental disasters and the resulting upheavals. These crises have a significant impact on society in several dimensions. In particular the education sector suffers, not only due to the repercussions of the current global situation but also because of the impact of these phenomena on the teaching-learning process. Such challenges reveal the vulnerabilities of traditional educational frameworks, intensifying seemingly insurmountable obstacles, such as limited access to resources and increased uncertainty about the future. These realities affect both teachers' and students' well-being. These challenges, similar to those that have occurred in the past, transcend geographic borders and impact various communities. It is essential to recognize the disproportionate effects they have on historically marginalized groups. The consequences of these situations are especially severe in areas that have long been affected by social and political conflicts and environmental disasters.

Our minds are under significant stress and pressure because of everything happening in our world. This stress is not just affecting one age group—it is hitting everyone. Sure, some stress can push us to do something about our problems, but lately, it has been getting a bit too much. When society expects too much from us, our minds, bodies, and spirits become overwhelmed. Anxiety can freeze us, making us more prone to falling into this idea that we can escape our problems by buying stuff, shutting ourselves off, or just mentally checking out. In our fast-paced, hyper-connected world, some people believe that friendship, love, and connection can be found with a quick click. While it may seem easy to establish friendships online, it's important to remember that reliable connections often take time and effort to develop. Being connected is less costly than being engaged, but it is also considerably less productive for building and maintaining bonds. In this challenging context, adopting a more holistic approach to education is essential. This approach should not only focus on academic aspects but also consider the social, emotional, and spiritual dimensions of our lives and our children's lives. By doing this, we can build connections that nurture strong and healthy relationships.

When stress becomes overwhelming, it can be beneficial to seek inspiration from sources beyond the usual ones from which we seek answers. The wisdom and insights of experienced individuals can help us explore new possibilities. One such insightful figure who can support us in our teaching efforts is Paulo Freire. His revolutionary principles can serve as a road map in these challenging times.[2] Although Freire's ideas are commonly inscribed within the adult universe, this chapter seeks to demonstrate how his concepts can shed light on educational endeavors, especially when promoting young people's spiritual and emotional well-being during these turbulent times. Freire's perceptive insights provide invaluable guidance for parents and other caregivers concerning how adults might avoid underestimating a child's fear, insecurity, or grief and support them in overcoming these difficulties by developing a resilient spirit.

Family: Place of Belonging, Differences, and Affections

In our interconnected world, people from diverse backgrounds come together, interact, build relationships, and form various types of families that are often evolving, transforming, and sometimes breaking apart. Regardless of how a family is structured, what matters is how relationships and bonds of affection are formed and how care and responsibility are shared among its members. Families are never perfect because, as human ventures, they always exhibit a dimension of lack, unfinishedness, and impermanence. Identifying and articulating what is missing is essential for building healthy relationships. The responsibility of raising children depends significantly on a support system that includes the extended family, social interactions, school, and faith community rather than just on the caregivers' abilities or shortcomings.

Nevertheless, this view of family relationships, emphasizing interdependence and mutual care, contradicts the individualistic mindset prevalent in our contemporary societies. Sometimes we try to meet our needs and voids with things that do not bring a sense of fulfillment. Life requires time to elaborate and organize our internal voids. It requires time to consider our needs and process our life experiences. Building relationships, even among family members, takes time, effort, perseverance, and compromises. However, because we live in a society that has made these relationships transactional—where people and things are consumed—we expect our demands to be satisfied immediately, which generates frustration about what we cannot obtain and intolerance for the suffering caused by unfulfilled yearnings.

As caregivers, parents, and educators, we cannot prevent the pain in our children's lives. However, we can accompany them in their suffering. We should walk alongside them, listening to their pain and concerns. Through attentive listening, discerning observation, and caring attitudes, we should be able to combine resources to assist them in dealing with life's challenges. Sometimes adults overlook or underestimate children's fears, insecurities, vulnerabilities, curiosities, or grief. By glossing over their feelings, we overlook the potential children possess to overcome their challenges, which enables them to learn from and with those experiences. However, when we acknowledge and validate their feelings, we foster resilience and confidence. Distress and anxiety are real; children need help navigating such turbulent times. Finding a balance between these two aspects is essential for nurturing their well-being.

A question emerges in this context: how can we raise children without hiding from or dismissing the pain but instead educate them to face those circumstances with courage and resourcefulness? One approach is to encourage curiosity, flexibility, and hope. Cultivating a sense of curiosity allows them to explore and ask questions about the world around them. Fostering flexibility helps them adapt to new situations and challenges with ease. Instilling a sense of hope empowers them to strive toward their goals. In the Freirean sense, hope is not just about wishful thinking; it involves the capacity to find meaning in life. It is an active and critical stance in which individuals recognize themselves as agents of transformation. This perspective allows them to envision a better future and take steps, however small, toward achieving the desired change.³ Encouraging children to express their fears, anxieties, and emotional struggles is an essential approach to help them navigate the challenges they face in their lives. By creating a safe and supportive environment for open conversations, we empower them to share their feelings and experiences. This not only fosters a sense of connection and understanding but also allows us to collaborate in finding creative and enriching solutions that can enhance their overall well-being. Through this collaborative effort, we can help children develop resilience and emotional intelligence, equipping them with the tools they need to thrive.

Promoting Emotional Resilience through Education

In *Pedagogy of the Oppressed*, Freire introduced the concept of "untested feasibility," which he described as a critical interpretation of reality, implying a learning process to deal with constraints and impossibilities that life imposes on us.⁴ Instead of being paralyzed, as when we feel fear and anxiety, we should feel motivated to take decisive action to realize the untested feasibility—that is, what has not yet been accomplished but which we can achieve. He argued that people frequently overlook their own potential and creative solutions due to societal conditioning that prioritizes established norms. This idea is crucial when addressing children's emotional challenges, as adults often underestimate how effectively kids can cope with stress, insecurity, and sadness.

Acknowledging and accepting children's emotions is a fundamental tenet of building resilience. Caregivers and parents can help children overcome difficulties by creating an environment where they feel free to be authentic and express themselves honestly. Furthermore, caregivers and parents must believe in children's potential to overcome difficulties and not project their insecurities onto them. In this sense, it is essential to listen to children through open dialogue, asking about their concerns without interrupting or trying to provide answers to questions they have not requested. Dialogue is a fundamental concept in Paulo Freire's educational approach, as it promotes understanding and empathy within any educational setting. Freire believed that dialogue offers a chance to reflect on our world and our perspectives on life's challenges. Additionally, it is through dialogue that we can gain insights into other people's worldviews. For Freire, dialogical education was rooted in love, hope, humility, and faith.[5] He said, "Dialogue cannot exist, however, in the absence of a profound love for the world and people. The naming of the world, which is an act of creation and re-creation, is impossible if it is not infused with love."[6] Therefore, encouraging children to share their concerns is essential, and it stems from our genuine love and commitment to their welfare.

Parents and caregivers can help children express their feelings by engaging them in conversation, reassuring them that these emotions are natural and valid responses to life's challenges. Embracing feelings as a natural part of life is vital for managing emotions in healthier ways. Consequently, promoting open and empathetic conversations with our children is key to supporting their development. By recognizing children's actions and perseverance, caregivers instill in them a belief that they can grow and learn from adversity. Through dialogue with other children, parents, caregivers, and trusted adults, children find possible ways to address these adverse circumstances. Caregivers can engage children in discussions, enabling them to brainstorm solutions to their anxieties and insecurities. This process fosters a sense of agency and empowers children to address their emotional challenges proactively.

In the context of emotional resilience, caregivers and parents play a crucial role in teaching children about emotions, coping strategies, and the importance of seeking support when needed. While verbal communication is valuable, it is equally important to recognize that children absorb and internalize these lessons even more from observing our behaviors. When caregivers and parents model healthy emotional expression and coping mechanisms, children are more likely to develop self-awareness, a critical aspect of emotional resilience.

Another aspect of Freire's pedagogy is his commitment to inclusivity and respect for students and their diversity. In *Pedagogy of Freedom*, he highlighted how important it is for teachers to consider each student's experiences and viewpoints.[7] Adults who care for children can agree that each child's emotional experiences are unique and significant. Sometimes professional help is necessary when feelings of fear or insecurity become overwhelming. Adults must be willing to help connect children with mental health specialists or counselors and work to eliminate the stigma associated with seeking professional assistance that is prevalent in many faith communities. A caring religious community should welcome young and old members and strive to overcome prejudice.

To help children develop resilience, caregivers and educators can encourage them to take small steps toward facing their fears and worries. These steps should be age-appropriate and gradually increase in complexity. We can encourage children to set achievable goals that align with their emotional challenges. For example, a child suffering from social anxiety may start by attending a small gathering with close friends from their community, gradually progressing to larger gatherings. This approach empowers children to take control of their emotional well-being and build resilience through action and control over their lives and emotions. By promoting emotional education and encouraging children to act in these ways, adults help children develop strength and prepare them to face life's challenges with confidence and emotional well-being. An environment that recognizes and values children's emotions equips them with valuable tools to face challenges with self-confidence and emotional resilience.

Empowering Children to Engage with Their Emotions

Children are not immune to feelings of fear, insecurity, or despair. Adults must understand the importance of these emotions in children's lives and address them. However, the reality is that some adults find this challenging because they have not dealt with their own emotions. So, it is crucial to understand the importance of not underestimating children's emotional experiences and to provide strategies for nurturing their emotional resilience. Acknowledging and validating children's feelings is essential to developing healthy emotional regulation skills, which are fundamental for fostering emotional resilience. When adults underestimate or dismiss these feelings, children internalize the belief that their emotions are not valid or real, and therefore they must suppress them. This can lead to long-term emotional and psychological challenges, impairing their ability to deal effectively with adversity and drastically affecting their cognitive development and social skills.

Adults should exercise emotional validation to prevent underestimating a child's anxiety, insecurity, or dissatisfaction. Children are more inclined to express their emotions when they feel understood, appreciated, and safe. For instance, when children express anxiety about an exchange at school, starting a new program, or showing up to a class that makes them uncomfortable, instead of downplaying their concerns, an adult could remark, "I understand that starting a new program can be scary, and it is okay to feel anxious; we all feel like that sometimes. What are some things that we can do to help you in this process? Can we write a list of scary things you have started these last few years and another list of things you are proud of?" With this approach, adults encourage open conversation while reassuring the child that their feelings are valid. Giving children the knowledge and skills to face life's obstacles while accepting their emotions is part of raising emotionally resilient kids.

To assist children in overcoming anxious feelings, adults can encourage them to express all their emotions, whether good or bad, by establishing a secure environment where they can express their ideas and worries without judgment. Indeed, children can benefit from adult guidance in identifying their emotional states and emotional triggers. To effectively support children in managing their emotions, caregivers can introduce a variety of coping skills. For instance, deep-breathing exercises can help kids calm their minds and bodies during stressful or anxious moments. Mindfulness practices, such as paying attention to the present, can encourage children to recognize and accept their feelings without judgment. Additionally, creative expression through activities like drawing, painting, or writing provides an outlet for emotions, allowing children to articulate their feelings in a safe and constructive way. By teaching these strategies, caregivers empower children to navigate their emotional challenges with confidence.

Children observe adults to learn how to live. Being a living example of emotional intelligence can effectively teach children how to deal with their emotions. While giving children support is essential, letting them face manageable difficulties is just as important. Allowing kids to make mistakes and learn from them is significant for their development, which ultimately helps them develop resilience. These children will be more equipped to express their emotions honestly, face life's obstacles confidently, and develop the emotional fortitude required to survive in an unsettling environment.

As adults, we are responsible for providing children with the emotional tools to thrive, express themselves authentically, and build solid foundations for their future. Knowing how to deal with failures is also a necessary part of life that teaches important lessons. Therefore, encouraging children to perceive failures not as setbacks but as opportunities for development and learning is essential. Emotionally resilient children tend to form more positive relationships, resolve conflicts effectively, and contribute to a harmonious social environment. Nurturing emotional resilience in children benefits their individual well-being and contributes to the overall social fabric.

Empowering Congregations through Critical Consciousness

A significant challenge facing congregations is the need to critically examine and understand the various structures of power and oppression that exist within society. These dynamics affect the broader community and profoundly impact children's development. Congregations need to critically analyze how factors such as socioeconomic status, race, and access to resources contribute to systemic inequalities. By doing so, they can better support families and children, advocate for social justice, and foster an environment that promotes healthy, holistic development for all young people. This introspective work involves recognizing these issues and taking active steps to address and challenge them within the congregation and the wider community.

This kind of critical exercise is what Freire calls critical consciousness. In *Pedagogy of the Oppressed*, Freire elaborated on the concept of critical consciousness, claiming that it is neither a gift nor a spontaneous experience but rather the consequence of activity, struggle, and a particular perspective we hold of the world.[8] This attitude of critical consciousness empowers congregations to recognize social injustices and actively work toward addressing them, embodying the principles of justice and compassion that underpin many faith traditions. Once we understand that education is not merely the transfer of knowledge but a means to transform individuals and society, congregations seeking to inspire transformation and spiritual growth among their members can use critical analysis to foster spaces where individuals are liberated from internalized oppression and empowered to contribute positively to their communities. Furthermore, Freire's insistence on the intrinsic connection between theory and action holds significant relevance for caregivers and faith leaders. This integration encourages individuals to apply theoretical knowledge in their daily practices and reflect critically on their actions and their impact on the communities they serve.

Applying this concept to caregiving and faith-based contexts, caregivers and religious leaders are urged to guide children and congregations to understand that faith is not passive acceptance but active engagement toward positive change. This dynamic relationship between theory and practice encourages individuals to reflect on their beliefs, critically examine their actions, and align their faith with social justice efforts. This holistic approach resonates with the teachings of many religious traditions that emphasize the inseparability of faith and action. Therefore, faith leaders are called to be agents of positive change in their communities by translating their shared beliefs into tangible acts of compassion and justice. Moreover, they can empower congregations to address societal challenges and embody the values of their faith in actionable ways.

Although these concerns and perspectives are genuine, some ideas may face resistance in certain religious contexts where traditional paradigms prioritizing rote learning or dogmatic approaches to teaching and faith are prevalent. Caregivers and faith leaders who are interested in embracing the ideas presented here may find it beneficial to engage in a thoughtful process of unlearning and relearning. This approach encourages the examination of existing assumptions and biases, allowing for a deeper appreciation of the transformative potential that liberating education offers.

Integrating these ideas into the educational and spiritual frameworks of faith-based communities requires unwavering commitment and collaboration. Caregivers, faith leaders, and congregation members must engage in ongoing dialogue, reflection, and action to cultivate an environment where faith flourishes and drives social change. To inspire our children's development, caregivers should embrace hands-on activities that reflect the values of community life. For instance, fostering open discussions about social issues within the family, encouraging children to express their thoughts, and involving them in age-appropriate community service projects can help instill a genuine and reflective faith. Faith communities can empower their congregations to organize outreach programs, participate in social justice initiatives, and create educational opportunities that align with transformative actions in the community. Although challenges may arise in implementing these ideas within faith communities, the potential for nurturing faith and contributing to social change is significant.

Caregivers and faith leaders can also help children critically reflect on their faith's ethical and moral dimensions by encouraging them to identify areas where their faith calls for action. One central element for young people is noticing when an adult does not walk the talk. That incoherence can be a significant impediment to their faith. For example, consider a situation where an older child observes adults in their faith community talking about kindness, empathy, and equality but also witnesses instances of exclusion or discrimination enacted by these adults. This disconnection between the stated values and observed behaviors can foster skepticism and disillusionment among children and youth, challenging the credibility of the faith community. Educators and faith leaders can respond to this reality by guiding children to reflect critically on their faith's ethical and moral dimensions. They can encourage open discussions where children explore instances where their faith calls for action and compare them to real-life observations. By fostering critical consciousness, children can better recognize social injustices and disparities, developing a deeper understanding of their faith's imperative to address these issues. This process helps bridge the gap between faith and action, nurturing a faith that is genuinely rooted in social justice and compassion.

Transforming Faith into Action

Educating children in faith requires intentionality, dedication, and consistency between words and actions. The outlined ideas provide a dynamic framework for caregivers, educators, and religious leaders to guide and empower children. This approach recognizes children's ability to engage critically with their faith and explore its relevance. Faith should not be a passive endeavor but one that calls individuals to engage with their beliefs and values actively. Caregivers and faith leaders should encourage children to act on their faith by participating in acts of kindness, service to others, and social justice initiatives. This active participation transforms faith from a theoretical concept into a lived experience. It enables children to see the tangible impact of their faith on the world around them, reinforcing the connection between faith and action.

An education in faith aimed at transformation enables the perception of human limitations and human potential to overcome challenges, finding possible solutions that can inspire positive changes in the lives of individuals and society. Caregivers and family members can illustrate the value of understanding that "untested feasibility" is not guaranteed but must be developed through collaboration between caregivers and children. In a troubled world that often overlooks the importance of our emotions and anxieties, where harmful interactions weaken ethical commitments, we must cultivate hope by supporting and nurturing our children's emotional well-being, enabling them to become resilient, compassionate, and loving individuals.

As adults, we are responsible for assisting children in fulfilling their needs for human development and spiritual growth. To that end, it is essential to use clear and accessible language, allowing children to understand and engage with complex ideas. However, we must also reflect on our teaching methods and our significant role as educators in their lives.

Listening attentively to children is crucial as it helps us understand their perspectives, thoughts, and feelings. Engaging in thoughtful dialogue with them not only fosters their communication skills but also helps us appreciate their inherent capacity for deep spirituality. By creating an environment where children feel safe expressing themselves, we can nurture their spiritual awareness and help them develop a deeper understanding of their beliefs and values. This dual focus on human and spiritual growth is crucial for raising resilient children who can confidently navigate life's challenges. And for us as caregivers, parents, and faith leaders, we must decide if we love our children enough to give them a "chance of undertaking something new, something unforeseen by us, but to prepare them in advance for the task of renewing a common world,"[9] as Hannah Arendt insightfully suggested in the opening epigraph.

Questions for Discussion

1. How is your faith community a support system for families? If it is not one, how might one go about being one?
2. How might the faith community create a different way of being from the individualistic culture?
3. How does your faith community engage children and youth in social justice initiatives? How is social justice taught to children and youth in your faith community?
4. By what processes can we attend to and engage the emotions of young people?
5. How can we help children to test the limits in safe ways?

Notes

1. Hannah Arendt, *Between Past and Future: Eight Exercises in Political Thought* (New York: Penguin, 1993), 196.

2. For those who may not be familiar with the groundbreaking concepts introduced by Paulo Freire, I highly recommend exploring his influential works. His most notable titles include *Pedagogy of the Oppressed*, which critiques traditional education methods and advocates for a more inclusive and dialogical approach; *Pedagogy of Hope*, in which he reflects on his experiences and the impact of his earlier writings; and *Pedagogy of Freedom*, which encourages educators to embrace the transformative power of teaching.

3. Paulo Freire, *Pedagogy of Freedom: Ethics, Democracy, and Courage* (New York: Rowan & Littlefield, 2001), 2–3.

4. Paulo Freire, *Pedagogy of the Oppressed* (New York: Continuum, 1997), 83.

5. Paulo Freire, *Education for Critical Consciousness* (New York: Continuum, 2005), 40.

6. Freire, *Pedagogy of the Oppressed*, 70.

7. Freire, *Pedagogy of Freedom*, 36.

8. Freire, *Pedagogy of the Oppressed*, 48–51.

9. See the epigraph at the beginning of the chapter.

References

Arendt, Hannah. *Between Past and Future: Eight Exercises in Political Thought.* New York: Penguin, 1993.

Freire, Paulo. *Education for Critical Consciousness.* New York: Continuum, 2005.

———. *Pedagogy of Freedom: Ethics, Democracy, and Courage.* New York: Rowan & Littlefield, 2001.

———. *Pedagogy of Hope.* New York: Continuum, 2007.

———. *Pedagogy of Indignation.* Boulder, CO: Paradigm, 2004.

———. *Pedagogy of the Oppressed.* New York: Continuum, 1997.

9

Dreaming in the Valley of Dry Bones: Childcare and Advocacy for the Undocumented Children in the United States

HEESUNG HWANG

DREAMers Walking in the Valley of the Dry Bones

Children, with their boundless curiosity, innocent laughter, and hopeful dreams, represent the essence of our collective future. In a world that often seems complex and tumultuous, it is imperative that we pause to reflect on the intrinsic dignity and rights of children, for they are the cornerstones on which our societies are built. Yet, in the shadows of our society, there exists a group of young souls whose dreams are often eclipsed by the weight of uncertainty and invisibility. These are the undocumented children, innocents who find themselves at the intersection of complex immigration policies and human compassion. Undocumented children, in many ways, embody vulnerability. Born or brought into a country without legal authorization, they navigate the "valley of dry bones" (see Ezekiel 37) filled with uncertainty, where the hope for a better life is often veiled in insecurity, fear, and exclusion.

The dignity of undocumented children lies at the heart of our shared values and principles. Every child, regardless of immigration status, has intrinsic worth and deserves respect, compassion, and protection. Children harbor dreams, talents, and aspirations that should be nurtured rather than suppressed. Working together for their well-being means not only recognizing their dignity but also promoting our own. Therefore, we must ensure that these children are not exposed to any form of danger and are provided with the necessary support and resources to help them realize their potential. We must also ensure that their basic rights and needs are met.

The Deferred Action for Childhood Arrivals (DACA) program, introduced in 2012, has been a significant development in the lives of these young immigrants. According to the Pew Research Center, 636,000 recipients benefited from the DACA program as of 2020.[1] Under DACA, recipients are granted protection from deportation and the opportunity to obtain work permits, allowing them to contribute to American society openly and legally. However, DACA has faced its share of legal and political battles, raising substantial questions about the rights and future of these children who are as American as their native-born peers. Children under DACA are also called DREAMers since they are protected by the Development, Relief, and Education for Alien Minors (DREAM) Act.[2] These DREAMers are navigating a precarious path filled with uncertainty and challenges in the country they have known all their lives.[3]

The right to an education, health care, protection from harm, and a safe and nurturing environment is a moral imperative, not a privilege. It is not a matter of charity; it's a matter of justice and protecting undocumented children's rights. The futures of these children are just as valuable as those of any other children, and they should not be put at risk because of circumstances beyond their control. As theologian Rohan P. Gideon asserts, "Without attention to children's unique suffering, theological understandings of 'liberation' and 'salvation' often narrowly exclude and diminish children, even though children are part of God's salvific plan."[4]

Faith communities can play a significant role in providing support and guidance to these children and families who face unique challenges in their lives, including legal, social, and emotional obstacles in the dark valley between the lofty mountains of capitalism, politics, racism, classism, and so on. Thus, this chapter examines biblical and theological perspectives on shared responsibility, child advocacy, and how parents and caregivers can assist DREAMers within their faith communities.

Biblical and Theological Perspectives on Shared Responsibility and Child Advocacy

Imago Dei

To understand the rights of children, theological educator Joyce Ann Mercer provides a solid theological frame. In her book *Welcoming Children,* she asserts that treating children as less important or less developed creates an issue of indifference and carelessness. Theologically speaking, children are "already fully significant human, whole-yet-broken people" from their birth.[5] As she explains, they are fully human but still in the process of developing. Their status as "in-progress" does not imply that they are less human beings. Children already bear the full image of God since they were made in the image of God.[6]

This theological concept of the *imago Dei* (the image of God) applies no matter whether a child is "legal or illegal, documented or undocumented, citizen or alien."[7] It does not discriminate based on age, gender, class, race, or culture. As Gideon asserts, "They [children] are symbolic assurance of the Covenant between God and the people of Israel."[8] Jesus' teaching echoes this idea: "Let the children come to me, and do not stop them, for it is to such as these that the kingdom of heaven belongs" (Matthew 19:14). This principle of not discriminating against children is also reflected in the United Nations Convention on the Rights of the Child, which states that "the best interests of the child shall be a primary consideration" in all actions concerning children.[9] We are also called by God to be advocates for the voiceless and powerless and to fight for justice and peace. We are to be the hands and feet of God as we care for his children.

Compassion and Justice: Welcoming the Stranger

We are commanded in the Bible to love our neighbors, show hospitality to strangers, and treat others as we would like to be treated. Reminding believers that they were once strangers in foreign lands emphasizes the importance of empathy and hospitality. We can apply these principles to the issue of DREAMers to guide our actions and advocacy, and they underscore our moral obligation to support and protect vulnerable immigrants.

Likewise, in Leviticus God sets the standard for us by commanding the Israelites to treat aliens as citizens of Israel; they were to love them as they loved themselves. They were aliens in Egypt, and so they were to love others as themselves (Leviticus 19:34). This commandment from God to love foreigners not only serves as a moral obligation but also as a reminder of our own shared history. We have a duty to uphold the rights of immigrants and refugees and to do so with love and kindness. We should strive to create a world where everyone can have the opportunity to work, live, and thrive in peace and security.

Deep Listening for Rooted Solidarity

Theological educator Patrick B. Reyes argues that to practice compassion and justice for children, we must cultivate and expand our theological imaginations. To love, nurture, and ensure the well-being of the next generation, he contends, faith leaders must engage their communities and gather stories from all walks of life to write a new, collective, sacred story.[10] This new narrative should be centered on how to create a world where everyone is treated with dignity and respect and where children can thrive—a world where justice and mercy are intertwined, and everyone can experience the joys of life.

By listening to one another's sacred stories across races, genders, and ages, we create a deep sense of belonging. The importance of listening deeply to children's sacred stories and discernment of our experiences—individually as well as collectively—is also stressed by Gideon because it is difficult for adults to understand children's experiences in a world dominated by adults' language. We should hear about their struggles, fears, hopes, and dreams. As Gideon writes, "Rooted solidarity involves a redefined responsibility of not just representing but also listening to children to a degree that, finally, what adults as individuals and as members of communities hear is converted into communities actively listening to children and creating spaces for their voices to be recognized and heard."[11]

Shared Responsibility

It is not just the responsibility of parents or caregivers to be involved in the lives of undocumented children as they move through this valley of dry bones and listen to these children's stories. In *Thus Far on the Way*, minister and child advocate Eileen W. Lindner points out that many adults claim to love children but are indifferent to their problems.[12] She also observes that the problem with modern American society is that it has relegated child-rearing to the private sphere of parents. She reminds us that the essence of Jesus' ministry was to the marginalized in society, arguing that it is, therefore, the mission of faith communities to stand with marginalized and suffering children.[13] In this sense, communities must share the responsibility of educating children to keep hope alive for the future of children and communities.

In *Seeing Children, Seeing God*, pastoral theologian Pamela D. Couture maintains that all children have a fundamental and equal right to be connected to a social ecology based on the family, community, government, and cultural identity that provides for the child's needs for survival, development, and flourishing.[14] As I proposed, the shared responsibility for raising children is only realized when the practice of child-rearing extends beyond the private sphere of the family to include the community and governmental and nongovernmental organizations, and the practice of co-nurturing becomes a mutually healing, restorative, and liberating experience. According to Couture, co-nurturing and resilience come from the grace of God,[15] "who executes justice for the orphan and the widow, and who loves the strangers, providing them food and clothing" (Deuteronomy 10:18). Our responsibility as disciples of Christ is to follow God's call and Jesus' teaching for the young, including DREAMers. We must be advocates for those who cannot speak for themselves, demonstrating God's love through our actions. We must be faithful stewards of God's grace and mercy.

Strategic Suggestions for Parents and Caregivers of DREAMers in Faith Communities

To protect undocumented children in crisis, it is crucial to develop a theology and practical strategies of child advocacy. In *Weaving a Just Future for Children*, child advocates Diane Olson and Laura Friedrich claim that "for Christian disciples, the mandate for child advocacy comes directly from Christ. Jesus demonstrated his deep commitment to ministry with and advocacy for children."[16] God's command to share the responsibility of caring for orphans and widows is thus directly linked to the exemplary ministry of Christ. These teachings remind us of the importance of protecting and advocating for children in crisis. We have all been children, and we have all been outsiders and strangers. No one is exempt from being made in the image of God, and we need to restore our sense of belonging through a community of rooted solidarity with God's children.

Supporting DREAMers in faith communities requires compassion and understanding. To develop and promote an advocacy project for children, Olson and Friedrich suggest four types of advocacies: education, service, public policy, and coalition building. According to them, education as advocacy involves various activities that raise awareness, such as learning about an issue, identifying resources, and writing a newsletter article to address the issue of at-risk children in the community. Second, service as advocacy involves creating or participating in programs that directly support children and families, especially those living in poverty, such as organizing a Vacation Bible School or a book club at a shelter for homeless parents or children of victims of domestic violence. Third, public policy advocacy entails activities that promote policies and funding to improve the well-being of children, youth, and families—for example, advocating for legislation to expand childcare for low-income working parents and proposing implementation ideas to policymakers. Finally, coalition building involves working with others to solve community problems and build productive relationships.[17]

These four types of advocacies are closely linked and will be most effective when they are working together. It is important to develop a program of activities that is based on the areas mentioned above in order to meet the needs of the community and participants. With this goal in mind, I recommend the following ways that parents and caregivers in faith communities can effectively support DREAMers.

1. Educate yourself. Take time to learn about the DACA program, immigration policies, and the challenges faced by DREAMers. Understanding the legal and social context is essential for providing meaningful support.

2. Open and nonjudgmental communication. Create a safe and welcoming space for DREAMers to share their experiences, fears, and aspirations. Listen attentively without judgment and offer emotional support. Be culturally sensitive to the unique experiences and challenges faced by them, recognizing that they may come from diverse cultural backgrounds.
3. Advocacy and awareness. Encourage your faith community to engage in advocacy efforts on behalf of DREAMers. This can include raising awareness about immigration issues, serving at a food pantry, supporting pro-immigrant policies, and participating in marches or rallies to share their experiences, fears, and aspirations. Listen attentively without judgment and offer emotional support. Be culturally sensitive to the unique experiences and challenges faced by them, recognizing that they may come from diverse cultural backgrounds.
4. Legal resources. Connect DREAMers and their families with reputable legal resources and immigration attorneys who can provide guidance on their specific situations and options. Organize "Know Your Rights" workshops for DREAMers and their families to educate them about their legal rights and how to respond to encounters with immigration authorities.
5. Pastoral support and moral guidance. Faith leaders and caregivers can provide pastoral care to DREAMers and their families, offering spiritual guidance, counseling, and a sense of belonging during challenging times. They can emphasize the moral and ethical teachings of your faith tradition that promote compassion, justice, and support for the marginalized. Help DREAMers understand that their faith community stands with them.
6. Community involvement. Encourage DREAMers to get involved in community service and leadership

roles within the faith community. This can boost their self-esteem and create a sense of purpose and can also help them discern and prepare for future careers.[18]

7. Scholarship and educational support. Explore scholarship opportunities and educational support programs available to DREAMers. Help them access resources for pursuing higher education and career goals.
8. Emergency assistance. Establish a fund or support system within the faith community to provide emergency financial assistance or resources for DREAMers and their families facing urgent difficulties.
9. Sanctuary. Explore the possibility of becoming a sanctuary congregation, offering physical protection and support to individuals facing deportation orders.
10. Achievement celebrations. Recognize and celebrate DREAMers' accomplishments within the faith community, such as graduations, job promotions, or community contributions.
11. Interfaith dialogue. Promote interfaith dialogue and collaboration on immigration issues. Partner with other faith communities to amplify your collective efforts in advocating for immigrant rights. Encourage DREAMers to get involved in community service and leadership roles within the faith community. This can boost their self-esteem and create a sense of purpose and can also help them discern and prepare for future careers.[19]

Conclusion

As Couture states, "Individual children die not only from lack of direct services for health and education but because national attitudes that devalue women and children prevent a child's flourishing from becoming a priority."[20] The role of faith communities in supporting DREAMers is multifaceted and deeply rooted in compassion, justice, and empathy. Churches and faith-based organizations provide sanctuary, pastoral care, education, and legal assistance. Moreover, faith communities can create a more robust and resilient support system for DREAMers and immigrant families by empowering parents and caregivers within their ranks, reminding us of the human faces behind the debates and the moral imperative to stand with those in need, regardless of their legal status.

Olson and Friedrich define justice as "an equal distribution of resources and opportunities."[21] For us as followers of Christ, sharing is not a choice; it is an obligation: It is our responsibility to share what we have with those in need, as well as to heal the wounds of our society. We must search for ways to redistribute resources and ensure that everyone has equal access to opportunities. We must work together to create a more just and equitable world. By recognizing and addressing the unique challenges faced by DREAMers, we take a significant step toward building a society that truly values every child, regardless of their immigration status, and upholds the principles of dignity and rights as universal and unassailable. Sharing the good news of God's grace and salvation to everyone, even in the dark valley of dry bones, is our calling. We must pay attention, pray together, and act for justice. Many DREAMers want to live a life they never dared hope for. They want to belong to a safe and supportive community where they can develop their identity and potential. My hope lies in the solidarity of faith communities that embrace Jesus' call to embrace all God's children so we can cross the dark valley together and rest in the garden of justice and peace. As we act with compassion and justice, I believe that the dry bones of fear, confusion, and separation will be animated by the breath of God and become a field of hope, dreams, and confidence for a better future.

Questions for Discussion

1. What role should the faith community play in protest movements concerning unjust action concerning immigrants?
2. In what ways is our church actively involved in advocacy and justice-oriented work? What role do we see these issues playing in our Christian witness?
3. How do we support members in our congregation who may be especially impacted by things such as immigration status or other such issues?

Notes

1. Jens Manuel Krogstad and Ana Gonzalez-Barrera, "Key Facts about U.S. Immigration Policies and Biden's Proposed Changes," Pew Research Center, January 11, 2022, https://www.pewresearch.org/short-reads/2022/01/11/key-facts-about-u-s-immigration-policies-and-bidens-proposed-changes/.

2. Joanna Walters and Amanda Holpuch, "Explainer: What Is DACA and Who Are the Dreamers?" *The Guardian*, June 18, 2020, https://www.theguardian.com/us-news/2020/jun/18/daca-dreamers-us-immigration-explainer. "Daca was a compromise devised by the Obama administration after Congress failed to pass the Development, Relief and Education for Alien Minors (Dream) Act, which would have offered the chance of permanent legal residency. The bipartisan legislation was introduced in 2001 and has repeatedly failed to pass into law."

3. Hillary S. Kosnac et al., *One Step In and One Step Out: The Lived Experience of Immigrant Participants in the Deferred Action for Childhood Arrivals (DACA) Program* (San Diego: University of California Press, 2015), 2.

4. Rohan P. Gideon, "Soteriology and Children's Vulnerabilities and Agency," in *Child Theology: Diverse Methods and Global Perspectives*, ed. Marcia J. Bunge (Maryknoll, NY: Orbis, 2021), 91.

5. Joyce Ann Mercer, *Welcoming Children: A Practical Theology of Childhood* (St. Louis, MO: Chalice, 2005), 251.

6. Mercer, *Welcoming Children*, 252.

7. Daniel G. Groody, "Crossing the Divide: Foundations of a Theology of Migration and Refugees," *Theological Studies* 70 (September 2009): 639, https://www3.nd.edu/~dgroody/Published%20Works/Journal%20Articles/files/TSSeptember09Groody.pdf.

8. Gideon, "Soteriology and Children's Vulnerabilities and Agency," 97.

9. UN General Assembly, *Convention on the Rights of the Child*, November 20, 1989, United Nations, Treaty Series, vol. 1577, 2, https://www.refworld.org/docid/3ae6b38f0.html.

10. Patrick B. Reyes, "Practical Theology as Knowledge of Origin and Migration: An Essay," in *Let Your Light Shine: Mobilizing for Justice with Children and Youth*, ed. Reginald Blount and Virginia A. Lee (New York: Friendship, 2019), 121.

11. Gideon, "Soteriology and Children's Vulnerabilities and Agency," 104.
12. Eileen W. Lindner, *Thus Far on the Way: Toward a Theology of Child Advocacy* (Louisville, KY: Witherspoon, 2006), 14.
13. Lindner, *Thus Far on the Way*, 28–29.
14. Pamela D. Couture, *Seeing Children, Seeing God: A Practical Theology of Children and Poverty* (Nashville: Abingdon, 2000), 43.
15. Couture, *Seeing Children, Seeing God*, 16.
16. Diane C. Olson and Laura Dean F. Friedrich, *Weaving a Just Future for Children: An Advocacy Guide* (Nashville: Discipleship Resources, 2008), 67.
17. Olson and Friedrich, *Weaving a Just Future for Children*, 68.
18. Kosnac et al., *One Step in and One Step Out*, 145.
19. Kosnac et al., *One Step in and One Step Out*, 145.
20. Couture, *Seeing Children, Seeing God*, 95.
21. Olson and Friedrich, *Weaving a Just Future for Children*, 30.

References

Couture, Pamela. *Seeing Children, Seeing God: A Practical Theology of Children and Poverty*. Nashville: Abingdon, 2000.

Gideon, Rohan. "Soteriology and Children's Vulnerabilities and Agency." In *Child Theology: Diverse Methods and Global Perspectives*, edited by Marcia J. Bunge, 90–107. Maryknoll, NY: Orbis, 2021.

Groody, Daniel. "Crossing the Divide: Foundations of a Theology of Migration and Refugees." *Theological Studies* 70 (September 2009): 638–67. https://www3.nd.edu/~dgroody/Published%20Works/Journal%20Articles/files/TSSeptember09Groody.pdf.

Kosnac, Hillary S., et al. *One Step In and One Step Out: The Lived Experience of Immigrant Participants in the Deferred Action for Childhood Arrivals (DACA) Program*. San Diego: University of California Press, 2015.

Krogstad, Jens Manuel, and Ana Gonzalez-Barrera. "Key Facts about U.S. Immigration Policies and Biden's Proposed Changes." Pew Research Center, January 11, 2022. https://www.pewresearch.org/short-reads/2022/01/11/key-facts-about-u-s-immigration-policies-and-bidens-proposed-changes/.

Lindner, Eileen. *Thus Far on the Way: Toward a Theology of Child Advocacy*. Louisville, KY: Witherspoon, 2006.

Mercer, Joyce Ann. *Welcoming Children: A Practical Theology of Childhood*. St. Louis, MO: Chalice, 2005.

Olson, Diane C., and Laura Dean F. Friedrich. *Weaving a Just Future for Children: An Advocacy Guide*. Nashville: Discipleship Resources, 2008.

Reyes, Patrick. "Practical Theology as Knowledge of Origin and Migration: An Essay." In *Let Your Light Shine: Mobilizing for Justice with Children and Youth*, edited by Reginald Blount and Virginia A. Lee. New York: Friendship, 2019.

UN General Assembly, *Convention on the Rights of the Child*, November 20, 1989, United Nations, Treaty Series, vol. 1577. https://www.refworld.org/docid/3ae6b38f0.html.

Walters, Joanna and Amanda Holpuch. "Explainer: What is DACA and who are the Dreamers?" *The Guardian*, June 18, 2020. https://www.theguardian.com/us-news/2020/jun/18/daca-dreamers-us-immigration-explainer.

Section III

In Search of Freedom: Caregiver Practices to Support Justice at Home and in the World

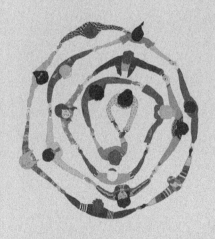

10

Young, Gifted, and Black

BARBARA FEARS

Introduction

Can you steal more than just something from the local store? For example, can you steal an opportunity from yourself or from a friend? Can you kill the spirit as well as the body? In what ways can you dishonor your parents? These are just a sampling of questions asked of six- to twelve-year-olds in the new members class I taught at Trinity United Church of Christ (TUCC), a Black church on the south side of Chicago, Illinois. We asked these questions of young, gifted, and Black children standing on the threshold of making a public commitment to an ongoing relationship with the Divine via baptism. These questions sparked intense discussion and rigorous debate and generated critical and creative thought about the Ten Commandments and the sacraments.

Most importantly, these inquiries led to honest dialogue about the children's day-to-day realities, such as doing their best in school, bullying, and obeying parental rules, thus grounding this religious instruction in their life experiences as advocated by educators Jack Seymour, Margaret Ann Crain, and Joseph Crockett.[1] I employed an engaged pedagogy and cultural artifacts as a curriculum to empower students and to instruct these burgeoning new members about the Ten

Commandments and the sacraments in preparation for their upcoming baptism. In other words, I used rap, TV shows, movies, art, literature, the documents of the church, and the lived experiences of the children to connect faith-based beliefs with real-world behavior.

Culturally Relevant Pedagogy

Having been introduced to the engaged pedagogy of cultural critic and black feminist bell hooks and seminary trained to be a student-centered facilitator of the teaching-learning exchange, I viewed my instructional task as sacred, or as hooks suggests, as sharing in the intellectual and spiritual growth of the students.[2] In addition, I was mindful that these students were instructed in school systems employing the banking methodology that was taught to the test (e.g., No Child Left Behind). Therefore, I employed a culturally relevant pedagogy reflective of theories and traditions specific to this age group and rooted in our church heritage, my knowledge of Black life in the United States (e.g., microaggressions), and Black identity formation.

Culturally relevant teaching uses student culture to maintain it and to transcend the negative effects of the dominant culture.[3] So we engaged the TUCC twelve-point Black Value System that articulated a commitment to God, family, church, education, self-discipline, self-respect, the TUCC Statement of Faith, which is comparable to the Nicene Creed, and the church motto that proclaimed us to be unashamedly Black and unapologetically Christian. We met in the chapel; however, we engaged the entire church decor (e.g., African print fabrics, Black art, and stained-glass windows depicting Black people) of Black creative expression and affirmation of Black life. In addition, I watched a week's worth of BET music videos in advance of each class to stay abreast of current entertainment news, to make myself more relatable to this age group, and to speak their language on topics that mattered.

While I provided opening remarks, historical, theological, and biblical contexts, and definitions of terms, students were invited to share their thoughts as recommended by several educational theorists rather than asked to recite data from rote memory as is the requirement of banking, which presumes that the students are empty vessels into which teachers pour knowledge. Rather than a top-down lecture approach, we dialogued. Students marveled that I knew the hottest rappers, and I rejoiced as I watched both students and accompanying adults turn quizzical expressions into inquiries about the material, then into smiles when students were able to put into their own words and social contexts the meaning of their pending baptism as we discussed meanings beyond the obvious for stealing, killing, dishonoring parents, and partaking of the sacraments. In short, these educational encounters provided these students with an opportunity to learn from the past and connect this new knowledge to the practical application of faith.

The Young

Researchers across a spectrum of disciplines have proposed educational theories for teaching infants to older adults. Many of these theories, however, were not developed with Black participants. Nevertheless, highlighted below are just a few theorists that informed my pedagogical approach to this specific demographic.

Philosopher, psychologist, and educator John Dewey (1859–1952) encouraged a student-centered pedagogy and thus advocated for teachers to create learning environments where students develop skills, solve problems, and contribute positively to society. In fact, Dewey was critical of the top-down approach of teaching where students remained passive learners. He favored instead an interactive learning environment where students connect knowledge with experience and exercise freedom as a means, not as an end.[4] Black children who are too often treated as either invisible or hyper-visible, which translates in either case as voiceless, were invited to share their understanding of the topic. For example, we asked what it means to kill someone beyond the gang violence on the city streets and in their young minds and lived experiences. Bullying became paramount, placing the adults in the room on notice of what mattered and what behaviors to watch for in the home that might be indicative of a problem at school.

Physician and educator Maria Montessori (1870–1952) proposed a four-part child-development theory. For her, ages six to twelve constituted the second stage, which she called the *conscious mind*, in which children desire to know, to learn, to help, and even develop a sense of moral responsibility and social justice.[5] This thirst for knowledge and developing sense of agency and social justice made discussions of honor/dishonor, theft, unfaithfulness, idol worship, and covetousness easy to engage with questions that allowed students to share their young understanding of the material in the language of their childhood experiences (e.g., cheating on assignments, betrayal in friendships), which also allowed them to note concrete examples from which to exercise responsibility and justice.

Psychologist Jean Piaget (1896–1980), like Montessori, proposed a four-part theory of cognitive development in which each stage must be completed before moving to the next. In his third stage (ages seven to eleven), known as *concrete operational*, children can problem solve but may not yet have the capacity to solve hypothetical situations. Fortunately, Piaget believed that the child's curiosity controlled his or her learning, and thus he encouraged teachers to create environments that promoted curiosity and challenge.[6] By asking students to think out of the box, to look beyond the obvious, to exercise critical and creative thought about ways we can violate our commitments to the Lord and thereby to ourselves, I created an environment of curiosity and challenge for these youngsters that enabled them to problem solve and to carry such behavior beyond the church's four walls. For example, considering "Thou shall not steal" as including stealing from yourself by not preparing for a test, earning lower grades, and ultimately resulting in the loss of college opportunity enabled these students to see the consequences of theft beyond stealing a candy bar from the local store.

Psychologist Erik Erikson (1902–94) also proposed a multistage life cycle. For Erickson, there are eight stages of life. These students fall into the fourth stage, School Age or Early School Years (ages five to twelve), where the basic focus is competence. A child at this stage learns to love to learn and to learn most eagerly those techniques that are in line with the ethos of production.[7] By asking students to explicate their understanding of the Ten Commandments and sacraments, students demonstrated a fundamental competency in the meaning of their baptism that served to build self-confidence and a positive self-image, which is also important in this stage, especially for children who are often overlooked and presumed to know nothing, which is different than expecting them to provide the one right answer from rote memory.

Educational and critical race theorist (CRT) Gloria Ladson-Billings (1947–) pioneered work in culturally relevant pedagogy. Grounded in CRT that asserts race is a social construct and that racism is normal, structural, and beneficial to the hegemony, Ladson-Billings's guiding principles for culturally relevant pedagogy are that (1) students experience academic success, (2) students develop and maintain cultural competence and academic excellence, and (3) students develop a critical consciousness through which they can challenge the status quo and current social order. For her, if students cannot apply, analyze, synthesize, and critique their environment and the problems they encounter, then they will not be prepared to be effective members of society. Rather, they will know only how to repeat what they have been told.[8] Black children can ill-afford to blindly follow the crowd, to be misinformed or miseducated, and to fail to think critically and creatively about their life experiences. In fact, to ensure their safety, life skills training begins at an early age. In other words, Black children are taught to be woke—that is, socially and politically aware, even at this youthful age. For reasons explicated in the next section, thinking out of the box on religious matters is necessary from the start. I wonder if a story of how this was demonstrated in your teaching would make CRT more real to the reader.

Growing Up Black

Report after report repeatedly shows that Black children do not enjoy the carefree time of childhood play (e.g., twelve-year-old Tamir Rice) or the presumption of innocence (e.g., Emmett Till). Rather, Black children are presumed to be older than their actual age, with no physical evidence to support such a claim. This age misperception, known as adultification, assumes Black children are older, know more or better, and thus deserve harsher punishment for actual age-appropriate behavior. In 2014 Yale University professor Phillip Goff and his colleagues reported that Black boys are presumed older, guilty, and less innocent than their peers. In one study, Goff and his colleagues asked 123 university students to assess the perceived innocence of children. The results indicated that for every age group after age nine (i.e., ten to thirteen through twenty-two to twenty-five), Black children and adults were rated as significantly less innocent than white children and adults or children and adults generally.[9] Goff repeated the study using sixty police officers, and the results were the same: Black youth were perceived as older and more culpable.[10]

Similarly, a 2017 report by Georgetown Law Center on Poverty and Inequality showed an anti-Black bias toward young Black girls ages five to fourteen demonstrating age-appropriate behaviors. In the Georgetown study, a mostly white female participant group perceived Black girls as more adult and less innocent of the same age-related behaviors as their white peers. For Black girls, such misperceptions have yielded expulsions and arrests for age-appropriate behavior (e.g., hairstyles, disputes with siblings). Such punishments are connected to higher dropout rates and increased risk of contact with the juvenile justice system,[11] which have the potential to create even greater economic and health impacts (e.g., employability, addictions) later in life. This age misperception also translates into Black girls receiving less nurturing, less protecting, less support, and less comfort after an unpleasant incident, having fewer mentors and advocates, and receiving fewer leadership opportunities.

Given the realities these Black youngsters face in the public sphere, the Black church becomes a sanctuary for these children who are otherwise seen as older with an emotional maturity beyond their years. It becomes essential, therefore, to provide these preadolescent children with a sense of identity rooted in their African and Christian roots and in their human/spiritual potential as image bearers of the living God. Are there specific exercises that can be practiced by local churches to provide a sense of identity?

Conclusion

Black youth grow up in a country hostile to their presence as evidenced by research revealing the practice and consequences of adultification and the practice and frequency of microaggression experiences, which professor and author Carmichael Crutchfield estimates can be up to five incidents per day.[12] Moreover, they are bombarded with print and broadcast messages suggesting Black intellectual inferiority. Such messaging can become internalized (e.g., colorism) despite our best attempts at affirming Black life. By employing a culturally relevant pedagogy with this demographic, I affirmed Black life, Black intellect, Black faith, Black creativity, and Black contributions, and created Black critical consciousness to relate faith to praxis. As students later expressed appreciation for the teachings from that class, this pedagogy gave youth voice to ask, "Why is this so, who said so, and on what grounds?"[13]

Questions for Discussion

1. How have terms such as instruction and education failed to allow teens to engage in their lived realities? What are some other pedagogical methods available to the faith community?
2. In what ways do our Christian education experiences speak to the lived reality of participants throughout their lifespan?
3. How does our church environment celebrate the cultural identities of our members?
4. How can our educational strategies support open dialogue and relational engagement rather than a banking model?

Notes

1. Jack L. Seymour, Margaret Ann Crain, and Joseph V. Crockett, *Educating Christians: The Intersection of Meaning, Learning, and Vocation* (Nashville: Abingdon, 1993), 12.
2. bell hooks, *Teaching to Transgress: Education as the Practice of Freedom* (New York: Routledge, 1994), 13.
3. Gloria Ladson-Billings, *The Dream-Keepers: Successful Teachers of African American Children* (San Francisco: Jossey-Bass, 2009), 19.
4. John Dewey, *Experience and Education* (New York: Simon and Schuster, 1938), 61.
5. Karl Aubrey and Alison Riley, *Understanding and Using Educational Theories* (Thousand Oaks, CA: Sage, 2016), 25.
6. Aubrey and Riley, *Understanding and Using Educational Theories*, 34.
7. Erik Erickson, *The Life Cycle Completed* (New York: Norton, 1997), 75.
8. Gloria Ladson-Billings, *Culturally Relevant Pedagogy: Asking a Different Question* (New York: Teachers College Press, 2021), 6.
9. Phillip Atiba Goff et al., "The Essence of Innocence: Consequences of Dehumanizing Black Children." *Journal of Personality and Social Psychology* 106, no. 4 (2014): 529, https://doi.org/10.1037/a0035663.
10. Goff et al., "The Essence of Innocence," 535.
11. Rebecca Epstein, Jamilia J. Blake, and Thalia González, *Girlhood Interrupted: The Erasure of Black Girls' Childhood* (Washington, DC: Georgetown Law Center on Poverty and Inequality, 2017), 9.
12. Carmichael Crutchfield with Denise Janssen, *Pressing Forward: Faith, Culture, and African American Youth* (Valley Forge, PA: Judson, 2022), 25.
13. Maria Harris, *Fashion Me a People: Curriculum in the Church* (Louisville: Westminster John Knox, 1989), 116.

References

Aubrey, Karl, and Alison Riley. *Understanding and Using Educational Theories.* Los Angeles: Sage, 2016.

Epstein, Rebecca, Jamilia J. Blake, and Thalia González. *Girlhood Interrupted: The Erasure of Black Girls' Childhood.* Washington: Georgetown Law Center on Poverty and Inequality, 2017.

Erickson, Erik. *The Life Cycle Completed.* New York: Norton, 1997.

Goff, Phillip Atiba, Matthew Christian Judson, Brooke Allison Lewis Di Leone, Carmen Marie Culotta, and Natalie Ann Ditomasso. "The Essence of Innocence: Consequences of Dehumanizing Black Children." *Journal of Personality and Social Psychology* 106, no. 4 (2014): 526–45, https://doi.org/10.1037/a0035663.

hooks, bell. *Teaching to Transgress: Education as the Practice of Freedom.* New York: Routledge, 1994.

Ladson-Billings, Gloria. *Culturally Relevant Pedagogy: Asking a Different Question.* New York: Teachers College Press, 2021.

———. *The Dream-Keepers: Successful Teachers of African American Children.* San Francisco: Jossey-Bass, 2009.

Seymour, Jack L., Margaret Ann Crain, and Joseph V. Crockett. *Educating Christians: The Intersection of Meaning, Learning, and Vocation.* Nashville: Abingdon, 1993.

11

The Dancing Mind of Parenting

ZANIQUE DAVIS

Introduction

As a little girl growing up in the Caribbean, I remember often hearing the popular idiom, "Do what I say, not what I do." I later learned that this idiom is not exclusive to my context but is also pervasive in many other cultures. Within this idiom lies an implicit notion that the recipients of such instructions must faithfully exude certain behaviors and principles without modeling the messenger's behavior. The problem with this is that, ultimately, children tend to model what is said and done by their parents or caregivers, either positive or negative.

Growing up in a rural area where the church was revered as a place of nurturing, many parents and caregivers relied on the church's elders, mothers, and other leaders to nurture their children. The church provided opportunities for children to improve literacy through the recitation of biblical texts and to learn public speaking. Children spent hours at church sharing meals and discussing future and current problems with one another, while parents spent time juggling two or more jobs to make ends meet. It was difficult for parents to carve out space for children to share their feelings or ask questions about God and the world around them. Some parents were restricted by time and a culture that did not welcome the active participation of children in various discussions, primarily with adults. Hence, our parents found it easier to instruct us to do what they said and not do what they did. They trusted that the church would help form our identity and understanding of the world around us, providing us with models to follow.

My desire to be intentional about how I nurture faith formation in my home is a result of my early faith formation and the importance of the church. Hence, as a Black Afro-Caribbean woman, now an educator, pastor, and mother, nurturing my two boys through faithful acts is an ongoing journey that requires me to model faithfulness for them to be faithful. Moreover, my earlier years allowed me to experience the role and importance of the church as a primary institution in nurturing my faith formation. It also sparked a desire to interrogate the role of the family in encouraging faithful children. More importantly, those earlier years nurtured the need to reclaim the family as a primary institution that models and teaches faithfulness in the home. To that end, this chapter's relevant question is: How can parents and caregivers embody faithfulness to help children and young people articulate and nurture a flourishing faith identity? Here, flourishing (in connection with religious educator Derek Hick's concept of reclamation) refers to children's and young people's ability to reimagine and embody a Christian faith identity entrenched in their culture, experiences, and traditions. Flourishing is evolving lifestyle that continually interrogates, deconstructs, reimagines, and refashions their sociocultural, historical, and theological realities.[1]

The Dancing World of the Church and the Family in Nurturing Faithful Children

Before we can reclaim the family as a primary institution that possesses faithful parents or caregivers to model acts of faithfulness for children, we must examine the influence of the church on the family and why the family needs to participate actively in modeling faithfulness and nurturing their children's faith identity. The dancing world of the church and the family points to a mutual collaboration of both institutions in modeling faithfulness for children and youth. This dancing world mirrors the distinguished theologian and womanist ethicist Emilie Townes's concept of the "womanist dancing mind."[2] In *Womanist Ethics and the Cultural Production of Evil*, Townes articulates an in-between space known as the dancing mind that invites womanists and nonwomanists to imagine and reimagine the possibilities of hope and justice against systemic evil.

Furthermore, the dancing world of the family and church relies on a communal imagination and articulation of what it means to be faithful and personal or individual agency in modeling a life of faithfulness. This dancing world is a collective and intimate space where the home should be the primary place that nurtures faithfulness, where children can learn about God and how to be faithful, while the church helps establish those beliefs and practices. Like Townes, my aim in exploring the dancing world of the church and the family in nurturing our children is to create a constructive imaginative space that works from a vantage point between boundaries of various contexts. Importantly, I endeavor to articulate theoretical and practical ways for all parents and caregivers to help nurture their children.

Therefore, such articulations and examples are grounded in my context as an Afro-Caribbean mother whose lived experiences are rooted in the social context of the marginalized and, therefore, understood through a liberation lens. Hence, the fundamental understanding of faith that drives faithfulness in my family is that our belief is entrenched in hope and an understanding of the nature and activity of God as a liberator and an embodiment of all things in and around us.

From my context, for centuries the Black church has played a vital role in the African American experience.

Religious studies professor Juan Floyd-Thomas argues that after the abolishment of slavery, "the historic Black church tradition became the most important institution among African Americans other than the family. Not only did churches fill deep spiritual and inspirational needs, they also offered enriching music, charity and compassion to the needy, developed community and political leaders."[3] Here the Black church operated as an extension of the family.

Similarly, Christian educator Kenneth Hill writes, "By the turn of the twentieth century, the Black church became the main school, community center, and political organization of African Americans. As such, it educated. The task of religious education was relating the faith to a new historical context and reconstructing it in light of the historic period."[4] Likewise, in the introduction of *Making Space at the Well*, psychologist Jessica Young Brown discusses the Black church's ingenuity in rethinking and reshaping their views on God, the church, and their overall faith formation after years of enslavement. Brown writes, "Black churches became a place of solace. . . . They began to form churches where they could worship in a style that was culturally relevant, and where they could discuss issues pertinent to the lived experiences of Black folks, as well as to fight against the prejudice and discrimination they faced daily."[5] The Black church's ability to provide context and content for families to experience the totality of their being helped many families combat circumstances that tainted their ability to actively participate in nurturing themselves and their children's faith formation.

Consequently, I encourage parents and caregivers to intentionally nurture their children's faith by first modeling faithfulness. At the same time, the church reinforces and partners with parents and caregivers to bring it to fruition. The family is the primary institution that provides for various needs, thus contributing to the holistic development of children. I am not dismissing the invaluable role of the church in nurturing our children. Instead, I am articulating a need for the church and parents to function as cocreators with God to model for and nurture faithful children. Parents and caregivers must cooperate with the church by taking an active role in this endeavor. In *Real Kids, Real Faith*, pastor and Christian educator Karen Marie Yust welcomes this collaboration between faith communities and families. Yust says, "Parents are the principal guides in children's spiritual formation, yet children need a religious community within which to experience God as something other than their friend or possession."[6] Although Yust emphasizes the church's role in children's spiritual formation, she acknowledges the significant role of parents and caregivers in children's faith formation. She later alludes to the active participation of parents and caregivers to ensure that children connect with faith communities that provide contextual opportunities to experience and encounter God through their realities.

Religious educator Ivy Beckwith describes the family as a primary institution for learning: "Family is the first place a child forms and experiences relationships. . . . Family is where a child learns language and motor skills and where she develops her first view and understanding of the world. . . . Conversely, family can also be where a child experiences her first emotional violence, neglect, indifference, and physical hurt."[7] Since the family is the primary institution that nurtures children's social and cognitive development, the family roles also extend to modeling faithfulness or a moral understanding for children to emulate. However, the reality is that some parents and caregivers encounter challenges as they struggle to engage with their children. Sometimes this struggle is due to a lack of support from other family members, extreme job demands, a lack of solid parent-child relationship building, or not having faithfulness modeled in their homes during their childhood. To that end, we must acknowledge the challenges that some families experience in modeling and creating safe environments for faithfulness. Early childhood and Christian educator Doris Blazer made this analysis of the family thirty-five years ago: "Family life in today's society reveals many influences that may be eroding the ability of parents and children to function as a loving, supportive unit."[8] The core struggles remain the same in our contemporary context.

Liberative Parenting: Exploring the Inner Landscapes of Parenting

The late Albert Bandura, a renowned learning theorist, developed a theory of observational learning that incorporated the key processes of modeling and imitation. According to developmental psychologist Wiliam Crain, Bandura saw the child as an "active agent."[9] Here, as active agents, children engage in the actions and languages of parents and caregivers to help make sense of the world around them. Bandura's modeling theory is intriguing because he demonstrated that modeling influences can alter children's thinking.[10] Here we see that parents and caregivers are children's primary teachers and, therefore, can strongly influence (consciously or subconsciously, positively or negatively) children's faith formation. Although I cannot entirely agree with certain fundamental principles in Bandura's work, his extensive studies on modeling through observational learning serve as an invaluable resource in raising parents' and caregivers' consciousness about our influence on our children's lives. I concur with Crain that "although most parents and teachers are already somewhat aware that they teach by example, they probably have overlooked just how influential modeling can be."[11]

Applying Jean Piaget's constructivist view about children's development to faith-building, Blazer writes, "Children's interactions with primary caregivers are essential ingredients by means of which young children will construct for themselves the meaning of faith. Not just what we teach but how we teach will influence a young child's faith construction."[12] Likewise, Yust concurs: "Children imitate the actions of those around them. . . . They will also ponder information they have gotten from trusted adults and then shape their actions to match their conclusions about that information. They enact what they have learned because they desire (consciously or unconsciously) to please the adults who taught them, but primarily embody their beliefs because that is how young children's minds work."[13] Therefore, raising faithful children relies on parents and caregivers to be conscientious agents in the family.

Being critically present with our children mirrors Paulo Freire's conscientization concept, which refers to a radical approach to education. This approach fosters a process of critical awareness that precedes action, wherein students become aware of the different issues around them and solve them.[14] For example, nurturing my boys sometimes feels beautifully chaotic, interspersed with divine interruptions. As Zayn, my five-year-old, and Zayd, my eight-month-old baby, reach various milestones as I'm responding to my job demands and meeting deadlines as a PhD student, life seemingly moves at an accelerated rate with little room to rest. Many days my hair is undone, the house is a mess, tantrums are high, and the timer is beeping away as I hurriedly fix meals for the family. Often it seems as if there is not adequate time to schedule prayer times, Bible study, or moments of undivided reflection. As the daily demands are high and strenuous to maintain functionality and productivity in our lives, embracing the possibilities of hope and the movement of God in my children's interruptions helps me complete the daily tasks and offers another way of being present in the home. Some days these demands become overwhelming, stifling my ability to see the divine interruptions and faithfulness in each moment. However, being intentional about my interactions with family allows me to model faithful practices.

The above description is an example of conscientization because of my awareness of the foreseeable and current injustices happening to and around children, particularly those who are marginalized. We are mindful of the children who do not have the resources and the support they need to process their emotions. Helping them make sense of the world around them helps me remain conscious about making my home a place where my boys can process the good and not-so-good situations around them.

As parents, we often become engulfed by the busyness of our days, which sometimes leaves little room to be mindful of our children's emotional needs. Hence, these faithful practices are undergirded in conversations through storytelling about our day's events and looking back to our past to connect with present and future endeavors. As a conscientious parent, modeling the desired acts of faithfulness offers my family a blueprint to carve out their unique ways of being and engaging in faithful practices. Furthermore, carving out such spaces allows us to unite as a family to discuss the things hindering us from flourishing faithfully and embrace ways to thrive in faithfulness. For example, parents can learn how to apologize to their children or work to share what they love and would love for them; this improves their parenting and reflects conscientization.

Moreover, nurturing faithful children to engage in deep faith for the present and next generation requires parents and caregivers to model practical faithfulness daily through self-awareness. Exercising great self-awareness is critical for effective parenting. It forces us to introspect, name, wrestle with ourselves, and ask messy questions. Revisiting our childhood experiences, dreams, and hopes can strengthen our connections with our children. Knowing our strengths and the areas we are developing helps us build the confidence to overcome insecurities, fears, or doubts about our parenting abilities. Being fully conscious of who we are outside of our parental roles means we continuously enter the terrains of our inner landscape to confront, affirm, and love our true selves. Doing so will help us create homes that offer our children healing, confidence, care, and love. We thus need to nurture our inner selves to be empowered to become the role models our children will desire to emulate.

Additionally, nurturing faithful children to engage in deep faith requires us to establish trust with children while engaging in meaningful conversations and creative interactions. For example, in our home, being in our season of busyness, we have created morning and bedtime routines with songs that facilitate positive parent-child relationships through playfulness and thoughtfulness. Instead of waiting for Zayn and Zayd to fall asleep at bedtime or to steal away early in the morning for quiet time, in this season of our lives, I invite them to be a part of our morning and bedtime devotions. Instead of shouting and becoming too frustrated when parenting gets challenging, like in moments of my sons' meltdowns, fussiness, or refusal to eat or sleep, I ask God to grant me enough grace to model the behavior I desire from them. I strive to be conscious of my emotional and mental aptitudes and how they can affect my interaction with the boys.

Crucially, parents and caregivers must know that faith does not just form into being for children. Instead, it is produced in parent-child and child-community relationships' social, emotional, and cognitive interactions. As the world demands attention to cultural and societal production, we must remember to make time in the everydayness of our lives to connect with our children. God moves through everyday actions, from giving baths, prepping meals, tucking our children into bed, and being present in our children's tantrums to spending brief moments conversing about our day. If we endeavor to be conscientious parents and caregivers, we will always witness God's movement through our intentional interactions with our children.

Additionally, creating space for intentional conversations with children shows that children's needs in faith development are authentic and valid. Like adults, our children seek to form effective relationships with graceful environments that provide a sense of belonging. They crave a sense of belonging, and this sense of belonging varies for each child. They want to know that their ideas are valued. They want to know that they can experience God on their own. They want to know that we see beyond their tantrums, fuss, mess, unresponsiveness, or reluctance to engage in varied activities and still care for their well-being, to love them in the chaos and busyness of our day. They want us to grant them grace when they struggle to complete tasks, to listen well, or to remember how to do things independently. Our children want to see a manifestation of our God that we share with them through our daily actions. Our safe space for dialogue nurtures critical thinking from sociocultural and philosophical to theological aspects.

During such conversations, I have garnered insightful lessons on how Zayn perceives the world around him and his understanding of God. During these social yet sacred moments, we reflect on how beautiful and divine our seemingly chaotic days were. These intentional conversations allow me to see how my son perceives me as a faithful person and mother, as well as the areas that require improvement in my children's nurturing and faith formation.

Modeling represents our intentionality to create space for meaningful dialogues and divine interruptions from our busy day to welcome our children's questions and faith needs. Yust argues that "children imitate the actions of those around them.... Our children add up, imitate, file away what they've observed and so very often later fall in line with the particular moral counsel we wittingly or quite unselfconsciously have offered them."[15] Hence, parents and caregivers must exude a life of faithfulness for our children to emulate. As parents and caregivers, we must play a vital role in ensuring that our children are encouraged to model behaviors or lifestyles filled with faithfulness. As they transition through various stages of development, they are still trying to make sense of God and the world around them.

I pray that God will grant us the grace and fortitude to be faithful parents and caregivers as we endeavor to raise faithful children. Please note that for many parents and caregivers, creating space for conversation during bedtime might be impossible or difficult. You could cultivate time for this bonding, self-discovery, and devotion to transpire at other times during the day. The important lesson is being intentional about allowing our children to ask the tough, messy, silly questions, to express their feelings, and to feel validated in that shared and sacred space. In so doing, we teach them through our actions more about the love and grace of God than perhaps any other way. Our faithfulness fosters their faithfulness. Raising faithful kids means being and becoming faithful parents every day. It means reclaiming the family as the primary institution that nurtures deep and critical faithfulness in children.

Questions for Discussion

1. In what ways can parents actively partner with churches to support children's faith development?
2. How can parents understand and capitalize on modeling and imitation to support faith development?
3. In what ways can congregations support increasing self-awareness in caregivers?

Notes

1. Derek S. Hicks, *Reclaiming the Spirit in the Black Faith Tradition* (New York: Palgrave Macmillan, 2012), 112.
2. Emilie Townes, *Womanist Ethics and the Cultural Production of Evil* (New York: Palgrave Macmillan, 2006), chaps. 1–2.
3. Juan M. Floyd-Thomas, *Liberating Black Church History: Making It Plain* (Nashville: Abingdon, 2014), 72–73.
4. Kenneth H. Hill, *Religious Education in the African American Tradition: A Comprehensive Introduction* (St. Louis: Chalice, 2007), 21.
5. Jessica Young Brown, *Making Space at the Well: Mental Health and the Church* (Valley Forge, PA: Judson, 2020), xiii.
6. Karen Marie Yust, *Real Kids, Real Faith: Practices for Nurturing Children's Spiritual Lives* (San Francisco: Wiley, 2004), 164.
7. Ivy Beckwith, *Postmodern Children's Ministry: Ministry to Children in the 21st Century* (Grand Rapids: Zondervan, 2004), 101.
8. Doris A. Blazer, ed., *Faith Development in Early Childhood* (Kansas City, MO: Sheed & Ward, 1989), 107.
9. William Crain, *Theories of Development: Concepts and Applications*, 4th ed. (Upper Saddle River, NJ: Prentice Hall, 2000), 204.

10. Crain, *Theories of Development*, 207.
11. Crain, *Theories of Development*, 208.
12. Blazer, *Faith Development in Early Childhood*, 39.
13. Yust, *Real Kids, Real Faith*, 150.
14. Paulo Freire, *Pedagogy of the Oppressed*. Trans. Myra Bergman Ramos. 50th anniversary ed. (New York: Bloomsbury Academic, 2018).
15. Yust, *Real Kids, Real Faith*, 149.

References

Beckwith, Ivy. *Postmodern Children's Ministry: Ministry to Children in the 21st Century*. Grand Rapids, MI: Zondervan, 2004.

Blazer, Doris A., ed., *Faith Development in Early Childhood*. Kansas City, MO: Sheed & Ward, 1989.

Brown, Jessica Young. *Making Space at the Well: Mental Health and the Church*. Valley Forge, PA: Judson, 2020.

Crain, William. *Theories of Development: Concepts and Applications*. 4th ed. Upper Saddle River, NJ: Prentice Hall, 2000.

Floyd-Thomas, Juan M. *Liberating Black Church History: Making It Plain*. Nashville: Abingdon, 2014.

Freire, Paulo. *Pedagogy of the Oppressed*. Translated by Myra Bergman Ramos. 50th anniversary ed. New York: Bloomsbury Academic, 2018.

Hicks, Derek S. *Reclaiming the Spirit in the Black Faith Tradition*. New York: Palgrave Macmillan, 2012.

Hill, Kenneth H. *Religious Education in the African American Tradition: A Comprehensive Introduction*. St. Louis: Chalice, 2007.

Townes, Emilie. *Womanist Ethics and the Cultural Production of Evil*. New York: Palgrave Macmillan, 2006.

Yust, Karen Marie. *Real Kids, Real Faith: Practices for Nurturing Children's Spiritual Lives*. San Francisco: Wiley, 2004.

12

Mentoring with Intentionality and Purpose: A Necessity in Caregiving for African American Adolescent Males

CARMICHAEL D. CRUTCHFIELD

Hey Black Child
Be what you can be
Learn what you must learn
Do what you can do
And tomorrow your nation will be what you want it to be[1]

A Story

On a cool fall evening about six years ago, my daughter entered my bedroom to tell me that she and her husband were planning a divorce. I was stunned by the news but more concerned about their three children, ages ten, eight, and two. I immediately thought about how my grandchildren would react to this news. I could not imagine them receiving it well, for they were very close to their mom and dad.

However, before my mind had a chance to run too wild, my daughter told me that she and her soon-to-be ex-husband had discussed it with the children. I could not imagine how they really felt. My daughter assured me that the two older ones were good, and the younger one would be okay. The two parents made an agreement that the permanent residence of the children would be with their mother. The father would take custody of the children during the summer months and all holidays.

As time has gone by over the last six years, I have observed from a distance how my grandchildren have been raised in a co-parenting situation. Their father is in the military and lives hundreds of miles away from the children. Through the use of video call technology, the children see and talk to their dad very consistently. And he has managed to take part in some of the most important events in their lives. For example, one fall he drove six hours to see his daughter be introduced as a new high school cheerleader.

I do not live in the same city as my daughter and grandchildren; therefore, I do not claim to know all the ins and outs concerning the co-parenting operation, but it seems to work out fairly well.

I often reminisce about parenting my two children when they were young. I think about the struggle their mother and I had in keeping up with their activities and nurturing them on a daily basis. I have found myself wondering how single parents raise children, for it was hard for the two of us to keep up with the many activities of our two children. My mind goes further back in time to when I was a child. There were seven of us, two years apart in age, except for the last two, who were twins. Our maternal grandmother lived with us from my first memory until her death when I was in my freshman year in college. She was the cook, the seamstress, the housekeeper, and the keeper of the children while my mother and father worked outside of the home.

My grandmother helped me to form some semblance of understanding about extended family long before there was such a word in my vocabulary. It was my grandmother who made sure we spent time with her son and daughter, our uncle and aunt, who lived hours away in another state. Visits with my uncle and aunt were always memorable because we were exposed to the big city, and what they had to offer was so much different than that to which we were accustomed.

Intentional Purposeful Mentoring

African American families are familiar with a myriad of family constructions. My contention in this chapter is that all those configurations benefit African American males through intentional and purposeful mentoring.

Intentional and purposeful mentoring of African American teenage males is designed to encourage young African American males to become successful Black men. It is an effort to promote education, respect, spiritual discipline, and responsibility. Additionally, mentoring discourages the use of alcohol and drugs, criminal behavior, premarital sex, and any activities that harm the body, mind, or soul.

Intentional, purposeful mentoring is designed to assist African American males to become aware, to plan, and to develop so they may reach the potential God has created within them to be positive contributors to society. This mentoring effort has the following goals:

- To increase self-awareness and self-confidence
- To develop a greater awareness and understanding of Afrocentricity and its implications for the family
- To develop a stronger sense of perseverance
- To increase community involvement
- To promote positive relationships with peers, girls, family, teachers, etc.
- To provide educational opportunities that include cultural and social aspects of individual development
- To encourage high career aspirations, to develop an understanding of the career requirements, and to inspire work toward realizing those aspirations

Intentional, purposeful mentoring is something churches can do, but it is not limited to the church.

The Context

Recently I attended the funeral of a friend who was a highly successful professional but fell on hard times as a result of a series of continuous bad habits and decisions that were hazardous to his health and to his marriage. These eventually led to divorce, poor health, and finally death prior to his sixtieth birthday. My friend's two young adult sons, who had been raised throughout their teenage years in a co-parenting arrangement, gave remarks at the funeral. I recall the younger son looking around the church sanctuary as he spoke ever so briefly, saying in a very strong and certain voice, "All of you raised me and my brother."

This young man is a college graduate and an Air Force pilot. His brother is a corporate executive who graduated from the United States Naval Academy. They had grandparents who were there for them as children, but the young brother's words at the funeral spoke of an extended family that included church members, school leaders, and in general, a community that did everything possible to see that these young men would succeed.

Not many would deny the important role parents play in children's lives. Nor would many disagree that extended family and "raising a child in a village" is very important. However, if these things are correct, and I believe they are, I ask why the statistics are so horrible related to the incarceration of young Black men. I raise that question not with the intent to promote, quote, or analyze statistics but to address possible ways to impact the unpleasant statistics in a positive way.

Mass Incarceration and Mentoring

As a young adult in seminary, I served as pastor of a church in western Tennessee that was only a few miles from a state prison. I accepted an invitation to go one evening to the prison as part of a religious service. As I interacted with the men, I couldn't help but note that the majority of those I had conversations with looked like me and were younger than me.

Writing the foreword to *The State of Black America in 2007* as a US senator, Barack Obama wrote, "In some cities, more than half of all black boys do not finish high school, and, by the time they are in their thirties, almost six in ten black high school dropouts will have spent time in prison."[2] Personally, I have witnessed Black boys suspended and later expelled from high school or quit at their own will, eventually on their way to prison.

For decades, politicians and civil rights workers, among others, have argued that there is a pipeline to prison from schools. This is a term often used to describe the connection between exclusionary punishments like suspensions and expulsions and involvement in the criminal justice system. Black and Hispanic students are far more likely than white students to be suspended or expelled, and Black and Hispanic Americans are disproportionately represented in the nation's prisons.[3] The Children's Defense Fund's Cradle to Prison Pipeline Campaign has championed a national and community crusade for decades to engage families, youth, communities, and policymakers in the development of healthy, safe, and educated children.[4] From my work with the Children's Defense Fund and my visits to prisons or jails for men, I have concluded that Black boys need not only extended family and a village, but they also need mentors because they face challenges as Black males that may land them in prison.

Michelle Alexander's book *The New Jim Crow* is helpful in our understanding of incarceration patterns and how they affect Black people. Her book is an argument that control of the Black population has been accomplished in the United States through enslavement, Jim Crow laws, and now through mass incarceration. Alexander argues that the United States imprisons a *lot* of people, and a far larger share of African Americans than white people are imprisoned. The excuse for this is the war on drugs, which has led to the arrest and incarceration of vast numbers of Black men. Crucially, Alexander argues that in the United States, Black men are arrested for drug offenses, whereas white men are not. Many reasons are given for this, but they mostly turn out to be spurious. Even though Black and white men are involved in the drug trade about equally, Black men are imprisoned more frequently for violating drug laws.[5]

A Mentoring Program for Churches and Beyond

I recall my grandchildren's father calling me several years after the divorce to ask me about programs or opportunities for his teenage son, who is my only grandson. I thought hard and long about my grandson and his lack of involvement in activities outside of school and church. I decided then to help him become involved in something worthwhile and of interest to him. I was thinking about a mentoring program that I helped to start that was taking place in the city where my grandson lived.

During my seminary years, I was fortunate to work part-time for an agency that addressed the needs of the community, especially the needs of children and families. That experience led me to develop a mentoring program by which mentees might have opportunities to serve, learn, and lead. In this chapter, I will not only state the case for mentoring but will give some thoughts about how mentoring might be accomplished by the church and other organizations.

The mentoring program I call Enlightened Males is designed for African American males ages ten to seventeen. It is designed to influence adolescents at a very crucial stage of their lives. During adolescence the external pressures of life, such as the need to be accepted, can lead to confusion. At the beginning of adolescence, most often, the need for peer approval is exhibited. In addition adolescents are dealing with competition and learning to cope in society. They are sorting out who they are. When one couples this psychosocial confusion with being a Black child in the United States who has a significant statistical probability of living in poverty, developing a positive identity is a difficult and challenging individual achievement.

Furthermore, mentoring is not designed only for those individuals who are having discipline trouble. It is my humble opinion that all African American adolescents would be served well in intentional, purposeful mentoring programs.

African American Males and Higher Education

The purpose of mentoring is to help mentees tap into the knowledge of those with more experience and thus learn faster than they would on their own. It is also an opportunity to grow their network and connect with leaders rather than only their peers.

Russian psychologist Lev Vygotsky offered a sociocultural theory of human development that is helpful in understanding mentoring. Vygotsky described what he called the zone of proximal development (ZPD). The ZPD offers an essential understanding of the distance between the knowledge one already has and the knowledge for which one is striving. The gap between these overlapping circles is assisted by the concept of the "more knowledgeable other (MKO)." This MKO bridges the learning gap through teacher/adult modeling or peer-to-peer learning (peer learning also engages social interaction). Vygotsky developed the concept of scaffolding, which also provides a way in which one can close the gap. Scaffolding refers to a method by which teachers offer a particular kind of support to students as they learn and develop a new concept or skill. Once the gap is closed, the scaffold is no longer needed.[6] The model of instructional scaffolding is also sometimes described as "I do. We do. You do."[7] In other words, the teacher shows how something is done, then the class practices together, and, finally, students work individually.

Intentional and purposeful mentoring places African American boys in the space of African American men who have great experience, have completed at least one degree in college, and have retired or are still working important jobs. The mentors are African American males who are simply asked to be present and be in conversation with boys about life. It is important to lift up finishing at least one degree to help inspire the boys on to higher education. For me, mentoring Black boys carries with it an emphasis on promoting and encouraging higher education through the presence of those who are college graduates, at a minimum.

Why is Black boys' higher education important? It provides young Black men with a healthy way to have a clear sense of who they are and what type of man they want to be, rooted in their own understanding of their values. Higher education teaches students to think critically in ways that most high schools do not offer.

The gap between female and male enrollment is widest for African American students, according to a 2018 National Center for Education Statistics report.[8] Considering that Black students are already underrepresented in higher education, this shows a concerning absence of young African American men in college. While some people may think higher education is too much of an investment of time and money up front, the benefits consistently outweigh those costs—especially for young African American men. I will explain some of the benefits for young African American men who attend college. I am not proposing a program of mentoring while Black males attend college but rather before college that inspires Black males to attend college.

My sixteen-year-old grandson was not certain about college until recently. Now he is beginning his junior year in a high school that has an early college component, and he is talking about college in ways he previously did not. I believe the intentional and purposeful teaching and mentoring he is receiving both in and outside of school has helped him to see the benefits of higher education. Among those benefits are expanded career opportunities, higher earning potential, a more successful transition to manhood, and improved confidence.

Higher education, in addition to helping to provide financial independence, may help young African American men gain a sense of living independently, away from the security blanket of home. Developmentally, they have the opportunity to shape their identity, reflect on their own values, and establish how they want to interact with others interpersonally. This provides young African American men with a healthy way to have a clear sense of who they are and what type of man they want to be that is rooted in their own understanding of their values.

Higher education not only teaches African American males to think critically in ways that high school does not, but it also assists in building skills that enable young men to make more thoughtfully informed decisions in their personal lives as well as in their academic lives. In college, students are taught to be self-motivated, responsible, and most importantly, open to learning from their mistakes.

Inevitably, young African American men are going to deal with adversity and setbacks in college, but it is important to allow them the space to figure things out on their own. Not having parental oversight challenges a young African American man to step up in ways that he hasn't previously. And as a result, he has the opportunity to transition into the responsible young man he has the potential to be.

Getting to class on time, completing assignments, and participating in group projects are standards that will be set in college. Like-minded, engaged peer groups provide a culture of support that help African American young men welcome this kind of responsibility. The structure of higher education allows for students to consistently be rewarded for putting in hard work. Having that feeling of self-assurance and appreciation of their abilities is important in building self-confidence. A sense of control and social support can be transformational for young African American men—purposeful living can motivate them to become the best versions of themselves.

Higher education also provides the opportunity for young Black men to enroll in classes and sign up for activities that excite them, without the structured limitations of high school. They can meet people from various backgrounds and cultures who have similar interests in addition to discovering new interests.

For decades institutions like the Centers for Disease Control and Prevention (CDC) have established that educational attainment improves health and life expectancy. Greater educational attainment is associated with health-promoting behaviors like eating fruits and vegetables and doing regular physical activity.[9] This is extremely important for African American men, who have a lower life expectancy than their white peers. Completion of higher education is key to having adequate food, housing, insurance, and other basic necessities for a happy and healthy life.[10]

In some cases, travel opportunities can be some of the best learning opportunities outside of the classroom. Through study abroad programs, alternative spring breaks, and internship opportunities around the country, students can make global connections. Traveling is a great way to grow as a person and to develop personally and professionally through meeting new people, experiencing different cultures, and learning how to go about daily life in a foreign place. No matter where a student enrolls, leaving what they've always known is the first step in discovering where they fit in the world.[11]

Curriculum of Mentoring African American Males

Mentoring with a purpose seeks to guide African American adolescents in a particular way of life. During group sessions with African American males, a curriculum is designed to engage the adolescents but always with the purpose of understanding the benefits of higher education. The curriculum considers the following.

The Adolescent Brain

It all begins with a desire to reach and teach adolescents. In her book *Secrets of the Teenage Brain*, educator Sheryl G. Feinstein elaborates on the teen brain. She asks, did you know that . . .[12]

- the brain, not hormones, is to blame for the inexplicable behavior of teens;
- short-term memory increases by about 30 percent during adolescence;
- the activities teens invest their time and energy in influence what activities they will invest in as adults; and
- teens are ruled more by their emotions than by logic?

With the understanding that the adolescent brain is under construction, the mentoring curriculum is designed to be presented in a way that does not feel like an institution such as a school. The space for mentoring intentionally and with a purpose becomes a space for exploration and development of self-identity. One of the elements of the mentoring curriculum is what I call "Put It on the Table." Participants are given an opportunity to say whatever is on their minds. This is effective for some but not for all. So, an alternative is to offer some community news and wait for reactions. Experience has taught me that the longer and more often we meet as a group, the more frequently responses will come forward. Field trips to exciting events, such as professional basketball games, help to open dialogue.

Violence

As I wrote in *Pressing Forward*,[13] "Young Black men and teens are killed by guns twenty times more than their white counterparts. Stories of violence from mentees are important. Experience informs me that these stories from mentees might include those of survival and avoidance of violence. Talking about the violence in their own lives might help to bring healing and education concerning violence.

Boy Codes

A mentoring curriculum for African American adolescents should challenge boy codes. Boy codes are unofficial rules that promote expectations of boys and often bring shame when they are not adhered to by males. An example is boys don't cry. William Pollack identifies four metaphors or imperatives at the heart of the boy code.[14]

1. The sturdy oak. This metaphor tells boys that they are to be stoic, stable, and independent, like an oak tree. They are never to show weakness, pain, or emotional need.

2. Give 'em hell. This imperative resembles the classic caricatures of extreme athletes and coaches, war heroes, and western gunslingers. It is the popular "boys will be boys" concept.

3. King of the mountain. This third imperative in the boy code demands that males achieve status, dominance, and power over others. It teaches boys to avoid shame at all costs, to challenge others, and to prove their worth by putting others down.

4. Be a man, not a sissy. This imperative prohibits boys from expressing feelings or urges viewed as feminine, such as dependence, warmth, and empathy.

In this curriculum, stories from men whose experiences counter these codes are the main sources to help Black youth understand that there is another side to becoming a man. I have found Black men who are readily available to counter these boy code myths with stories from their own lives.

Racism

Any curriculum designed for African American adolescents must consider the effects of racism. African American adolescents in the United States encounter racism almost every day.

Most people think of racism as a social issue. But it is a health issue too. Being confronted with racist acts can hurt a teen's mental health. It can make people question their self-worth. Scientists have even linked signs of depression in Black adolescents to their experiences with racism.[15]

Presence

The last consideration of the curriculum is presence. I have learned by mentoring intentionally and with purpose that when a group of African American males are present with African American adolescents, their presence speaks volumes. At times during a mentoring session, I have asked all the adult men to say something about their college and work experience.

Conclusion

African American families are constructed in various ways. Single mothers are often maligned and even accused of being incapable of raising African American males. The truth is many successful males were raised by single parents. I argue that all family constructs benefit from intentional, purposeful mentoring, especially when African American males are involved. This is largely due to the high risk that African American males face in becoming a part of the school-to-prison pipeline. Intentional, purposeful mentoring includes inspiring African American males to aspire to become involved in higher education as a means of becoming productive citizens.

I have designed a mentoring program that has proven to be of benefit to African American families. The curriculum addresses some of the critical factors that African American males are called to face. It is not designed specifically for use by local congregations, but it can be used in that way. My experience is that it provides an opportunity for civic organizations, including Black fraternities, to be involved in intentional purposeful mentoring.

Questions for Discussion

1. In what ways can we support the future-orientation of teens and help them prepare to thrive in adulthood?
2. What groups in our congregations might need intentional support and encouragement to combat systemic challenges?
3. What venues can be used to support mentoring relationships between teens and willing adults?
4. How might congregations and youth teachers and leaders be helped by knowing more about the adolescent brain? What other resources might be helpful?

Notes

1. "Hey Black Child," Marian Cheek Jackson Center, 2017, https://jacksoncenter.info/wp-content/uploads/2021/01/Hey-Black-Child.pdf. This poem was made during and for the Harlem Renaissance when Black people moved north seeking better opportunities.

2. Barack Obama, foreword to *The State of Black America 2007: Portrait of the Black Male*, ed. Stephanie J. Jones (New York: Beckham, 2007), 11.

3. Andrew Bacher-Hicks et al., "Proving the School-to-Prison Pipeline," *Education Next* 21, no. 4 (Fall 2021): 52–57, https://www.educationnext.org/proving-school-to-prison-pipeline-stricter-middle-schools-raise-risk-of-adult-arrests/.

4. The Children's Defense Fund has an extensive fact sheet concerning the pipeline. Visit https://www.childrensdefense.org/wp-content/uploads/2018/08/cradle-to-prison-pipeline-overview-fact-sheet-2009.pdf.

5. Michelle Alexander, *The New Jim Crow* (New York: New Press, 2020), 120ff.

6. Saul McLeod, "Vygotsky's Sociocultural Theory of Cognitive Development," *Simply Psychology*, updated August 9, 2024, https://www.simplypsychology.org/vygotsky.html.

7. "What Is Scaffolding in Education and How Is It Applied?," Grand Canyon University, September 19, 2023, https://www.gcu.edu/blog/teaching-school-administration/what-scaffolding-in-education-how-applied#h-what-is-scaffolding-in-education.

8. "Status and Trends in the Education of Racial and Ethnic Groups 2018," IES, National Center for Educational Statistics, accessed September 22, 2023, https://nces.ed.gov/pubs2019/2019038.pdf.

9. John Mirowsky and Catherine E. Ross, "Education, Cumulative Health, and Advantages" *Springer Nature Link* 30 (December 2005): 27–62, https://link.springer.com/article/10.1007/BF02681006.

10. Richard V. Reeves et al., "The Challenges Facing Black Men—and the Case for Action," Brookings, November 19, 2020, https://www.brookings.edu/articles/the-challenges-facing-black-men-and-the-case-for-action/.

11. Reeves et al., "The Challenges Facing Black Men."

12. Sheryl G. Feinstein, *Secrets of the Teenage Brain: Research-Based Strategies for Reaching and Teaching Today's Adolescents* (Thousand Oaks, CA: Corwin, 2009), 3.

13. Carmichael Crutchfield with Denise Janssen, *Pressing Forward: Faith, Culture, and African American Youth* (Valley Forge, PA: Judson, 2022), 57.

14. William Pollack, *Real Boys: Rescuing Our Sons from the Myths of Boyhood* (New York: Henry Holt, 1998).

15. Bethany Brookshire, "Suffering from Racist Acts Can Prompt Black Teens to Constructive Action," *Science News Explores*, December 7, 2020, https://www.snexplores.org/article/racism-black-teens-action-resilience-social-justice.

13

Conscious Parenting as Liberative Parenting

JESSICA YOUNG BROWN

What Is Conscious Parenting?

As a teacher, consultant, and therapist, I spend a lot of time thinking about what it means to create open spaces for people to come into themselves. Many of my colleagues in this volume have outlined the fallacies associated with the banking model of education and how this reinforces a top-down approach to education that turns children (people in general) into repetitive robots, able to parrot what has been poured into them. However, humanistic and liberative educational models offer frameworks that privilege subjective experience as the primary tool for learning. Humanistic theorists such as Abraham Maslow and Carl Rogers set self-actualization as the highest pinnacle of human success—a "mountaintop" experience that is categorized by a deep knowledge of one's self and one's purpose in the world.[1] Theologian James Fowler applied this phenomenological reality specifically to our religious and spiritual reality. He coined the term *universalizing faith* to represent a way of doing faith that is simultaneously sure of one's own understanding of the Divine as well as accepting of and receptive to the experiences of others.[2]

I had built a career based on creating these open spaces for my students and my clients, arguably with much success. I felt an openness as an educator to let people show up as they were, to take what I offered them and hold space for them to chew on it, mold it, critique it, and ultimately refashion it into something that worked for them. I assumed autonomy for them that allowed me to sit back and watch the process unfold.

Then I became a parent. After the first few months of infancy, my son started wanting to do things. So many things. Things that would hurt him. Things that inconvenienced me. Things that made me laugh and brought me joy. As he started to become more mobile, I felt this intense desire to protect him at all costs, but he seemed to thrive in the precarity of danger, doing things like jumping off the stairs and finding the most thrill-seeking things to get into. Then he started talking. And he never stopped talking. He took any opportunity to tell me what he wanted and did not want. He asked questions. So many questions! He was a person. I know this sounds silly, but somehow I was not prepared for his personhood. My models of parenting, despite my training and liberative teaching practices, centered on protecting him and keeping him safe but also on molding him into the kind of human I envisioned. He quickly taught me that he was already prepared to show up as his own kind of human, and I learned that the rubric I had of parenting would not work. So what to do instead?

Around the time my son entered toddlerhood, I began to grapple with the concept of transgenerational trauma, particularly as it shows up in Black families. As a Black woman, I have always felt called to work with Black individuals and communities. Doing this work in a meaningful way left me realizing that our traditional psychological theories are mostly inefficient in tackling the complexities of the Black experience in America. Social worker and educator Joy DeGruy Leary's *Post-Traumatic Slave Syndrome* (PTSS) provided the missing piece to the puzzle. In her seminal work, DeGruy Leary outlines how Black folks in America are living with and recreating the trauma of chattel slavery in our interactions with one another and with the world.[3]

I quickly recognized how the dynamics of emotional suppression, family secrets, and persistent fears about safety showed up in my clinical practice. But what did this mean for me as a parent? In what ways was I unconsciously recreating oppressive practices in the way I parented? I was forced to ask myself a critical question then and every day since then: Am I raising my children for slavery or for freedom? When I attempted to discipline my son out of a tantrum rather than helping him build the language and embodied knowledge for understanding his emotions, was I teaching him to recreate the violent legacy of stoicism that pulls Black people away from honoring their humanity? When I used "because I said so" as a rationale for my decisions rather than explaining my thought process, was I discouraging the critical thought that would lead him to be an adult who was willing to challenge the status quo and advocate for himself? When I made his world smaller to assuage my own constant fear about his safety as a Black boy who would eventually become a Black man, was I reinforcing limits on him that I hoped he would one day surpass? I was. So, I was forced into a point of reckoning: Was I raising my child for slavery or for freedom?

My search to untangle myself from the way transgenerational trauma impacted my parenting led me to the paradigm of conscious parenting. This way of parenting is a specialization of gentle, positive parenting that focuses specifically on parenting as a tool for reparative justice. Conscious parenting is a way of recognizing the autonomy of children and the responsibility of parents to nurture their children in a way that actively works to combat systems of oppression in an evil world. For me, another critical component became relevant. With the language we use in the church about God as a parent, how does my parenting do God justice? This conviction demands my thoughtfulness and attention to the way I treat my children but also to the way I treat all people. It becomes a part of the way I live out my Christian witness.

Yolanda Williams, a conscious parenting coach and activist, provides the following Ten Tenets of Conscious Parenting in a public social media group where she educates Black parents on conscious parenting.[4] How can these tenets provide a structure for liberative parenting that helps children to connect with themselves and the Divine?

1. We discipline our children with respect, not violence or shame.
2. We acknowledge our traumas (childhood + beyond) and do the work to identify how they impact our parenting.
3. We are mindful of our triggers, mindset, and mood. We understand that how we respond to our children is our own responsibility.
4. We take care of ourselves so that we can parent from a place of peace and intention.
5. We seek knowledge of child development and age-appropriate behavior rooted in science, not our own expectations or the traditions of others.
6. We model the respectful behavior, language, and actions that we wish our children to exhibit.
7. We provide clear structure, discipline, and boundaries when necessary. Moreover, through freedom and autonomy, we encourage our children to make their own choices.
8. We foster a safe environment at home for our children to express their thoughts and emotions. We view undesirable behavior as an opportunity to help our children develop the skills they need.
9. We recognize that it is our role as parents to nurture and not dictate the gifts already inside of our children.

10. As we continue to grow and evolve in parenthood, we also remember to treat ourselves with compassion and love.

Conscious Parenting as Embodiment of an Ethic of Liberation Theology

Williams's first, sixth, seventh, and ninth tenets mirror some of the primary ideas of liberation theology frameworks. In James Cone's words, "... a Black theology of liberation is basically an interpretation of the Gospel that affirms Black people's struggle for justice and their struggle to be Black."[5] It is an unapologetic affirmation of our personhood, seeing ourselves as made in the image of God. If we are all made in God's image, adults and children alike, this demands that we treat children as they are, as manifestations of the Divine. This special treatment is not to be earned or doled out as a reward for good behavior. It is a birthright.

For those of us who care for children from oppressed and marginalized communities, this manner of parenting is also an intentional and holistic dismantling of the oppressive systems that we are exposed to in the world. Our figurative and literal spaces then become what Fowler called "zones of liberation" that help us to be free.[6] Liberation theologies remind us that God is on the side of the oppressed, but also that we can partner with God to participate in the destruction of oppressive systems. Our emotionally safe relational spaces provide a revolutionary antidote to a violent world. To treat my children as if they embody the *imago Dei* is to demonstrate in word and deed that they are inherently good, that they are inherently worthy of my love, care, and respect without qualification or condition. Through an emancipatory lens, it is to be intentional in my awareness that this message is categorically different from the ones they may get elsewhere in the world. It is to give them a felt sense of unconditional love and regard so that love and liberation can become the litmus test by which they navigate the world. This safe home base then is a jumping-off point for responding to and fighting against an oppressive world.

This framework deliberately combats what I call a "works righteousness" framework that demands that we need to earn our place in family, community, or faith by doing good things because our goodness is nonnegotiable. Departures from good behaviors do not call our inherent worthiness into question. This means recognizing that my children's "bad behaviors" are about their inability to do what I am asking them to do, not their willful disobedience or rebellion. Privileging their goodness also allows me to correct and redirect them with gentleness and empathy rather than with anger.

Conscious Parenting as Conscientization

Psychologist Maureen O'Hara argues that both Carl Rogers and Paulo Freire envision a world where a free and critically aware environment leads to the process of conscientization: a building of a critical consciousness of the realities in the world, which ultimately leads to emancipation,[7] necessary to hold space for the freedom and liberation of children. For us to provide a liberative space for our kids, we must become aware of the ways in which we have been impacted by and recreate oppressive systems in our own lives. This liberative space requires that we ask critical questions such as these: How has my childhood trauma rewired my brain and shaped how I experience and respond to conflict or uncertainty? How do my experiences of microaggressions in response to my Black womanhood in work environments shape the way I police my Black daughter's dress, hair, and behavior? How does my concern about racist violence directed at my Black son impact the extent to which I allow him to show emotion or disagree with me?

In other words, liberation necessarily requires introspection. A major assumption of DeGruy Leary's *Post-Traumatic*

Slave Syndrome and Freire's *Pedagogy of the Oppressed* is that oppressed people take on the tactics of oppression to survive.[8] Conscientization is a necessary process for our freedom. This process requires that we disentangle ourselves from our participation in oppressive systems so that we can work to break them down. In the context of our caregiving for children, this also means giving ourselves permission to constantly critique the expectations we have of children. Is this child misbehaving, or are they exhibiting developmentally appropriate behaviors? In what ways do our fears and concerns as adults have the effect of unintentionally shrinking the space children have to dream, explore, and feel?

Conscious Parenting as a Model for Grace

Williams's fourth, eighth, and tenth tenets put into praxis a way of relating to ourselves and others that can be intrinsically tied to a Christlike way of living in the world. To acknowledge that we are responsible for how we treat ourselves and our children mirrors Jesus' command that we love our neighbor as ourselves. To build a safe home environment is to execute Jesus' admonition, "Let the children come to me; do not stop them, for it is to such as these that the kingdom of God belongs" (Mark 10:14). It is to recognize that children deserve space to explore, be free, and grow. These conditions, not ones in which we control our children and demand their submission, allow the space for them to understand and internalize their faith in ways that will last longer than our physical presence in our lives. This process is an opportunity to model what we hope our children will embody as they grow: love, openness, justice, and righteousness.

Just as our religious systems must address sin, our parenting must take a stance on right and wrong. To parent consciously is not to say that anything and everything is appropriate. Certain things need to be addressed because they are dangerous, out of line with our family values, or against rules that help society to function well. An often-uttered refrain in some Christian communities is "Spare the rod, spoil the child," a nod to Proverbs 13:24. Many interpret that to mean that harsh discipline, sometimes including physical punishment, is necessary to keep our children in line and out of trouble. Stacy Patton, in her book *Spare the Kids: Why Whupping Children Won't Save Black America*, argues that this passage refers to discipline rather than punishment. The rod used by shepherds alluded to in this passage was a boundary to guide sheep in the right direction and keep them out of trouble, rather than a weapon meant to beat sheep into submission.[9]

Patton and other theorists like DeGruy Leary argue that corporal punishment and other restrictive or harsh parenting strategies are a reenactment of trauma-inducing tactics used to subdue African people during chattel slavery and to terrorize Black Americans in the Jim Crow South. Thus, to consciously parent is to focus on discipline as direction and guidance rather than simply punishing bad behavior. Conscious parenting operates on the assumption that all behaviors, even "bad" ones, are simply an articulation of a need or an expression of an area of growth. It is akin to the central salvific message—we need help from God to do the right thing. Grace abounds so that we can begin each new day as an opportunity to live out our call. The reality is that we, as parents, will also do wrong and mess up. Being in a healthy, authentic relationship means atoning and apologizing for those errors and making a commitment to do better in the future. If we commit to getting curious about ourselves and extending grace as we figure things out, we can model a nonpunitive learning process for our children that helps them to avoid being crippled by shame and doubt when they make mistakes.

The Practice of Liberative Parenting

Parenting and caregiving in any form is hard work. While there are moments of joy and wonder, most of us also recognize that to be responsible for the development of a child is a great responsibility that we should not take lightly. We often build ideas in our heads about who and what we want our children to be and what path they should take. Well-intentioned though we may be, the ultimate expression of courage and emancipation is to focus less on molding the child and focus more on fostering an environment where they can grow into who and what they are called to be. If we truly believe that they are made in God's image, born with inherent goodness, then allowing them to chart their own path will lead to a holy journey, even if (when) it contains twists and turns.

As I seek to be a conscious parent, I recognize that it would be easier just to boss my kids around. But I constantly have to ask myself, "What kind of adults do I see the potential for them to become?" This requires a certain humility that many of us, as caregivers, are not encouraged to embody. I remember one particular time when, after a disciplinary encounter, my son came to me and said, "Mom, it really made me mad when you did that." I was convinced that I was right, and it would have been easy enough to shut him down. But I also know that I want to raise a person who is able to advocate for himself and others and who calls out injustice when he sees it. So, in that moment, I chose curiosity over condemnation: "I'm sorry that you're feeling upset. What about our conversation made you mad?" We went on to have a discussion about the tones we used, a misunderstanding about what our issues were, and his sense that I hadn't listened to his side of the story. Because he felt comfortable telling me how he felt, he had an opportunity to better understand the rationale behind the choice I made as his parent, and I understood a new way to discipline him that he could take in better. It took more time and was more work, but it also was a step in equipping him to be the person he has the capacity to be. If he can address his faith walk with the thoughtfulness, authenticity, and courage he exhibited in this encounter, we've done a good thing together.

Questions for Discussion

1. What term do you use as a parent or caregiver, *punishment* or *discipline*? What is the driving difference between the two terms?
2. What do you see as the strong points of liberative parenting, and what are some challenges?
3. In what ways have our personal experiences impacted our caregiving beliefs and strategies?
4. What strategies can congregations use to intentionally combat systemic barriers and oppressions faced by young people?

Notes

1. Abraham H. Maslow, *Toward a Psychology of Being* (New York: Van Nostrand, 1968).
2. W. James Fowler, *Stages of Faith* (New York: Harper Collins, 1981).
3. Joy DeGruy Leary, *Post-Traumatic Slave Syndrome: America's Legacy of Enduring Injury and Healing* (Milwaukie, OR: Uptone, 2005).
4. Yolanda A Williams, "Conscious Parenting for the Culture: Facebook," Conscious Parenting for the Culture Public Group, accessed March 8, 2024, https://www.facebook.com/groups/CPTime/learning_content/?filter=347585155799334.
5. James D. Kirylo and James H. Cone, "Chapter Eight: Paulo Freire, Black Theology of Liberation, and Liberation Theology: A Conversation with James H. Cone," *Counterpoints* 385 (2011): 195–212, http://www.jstor.org/stable/42980930, 199.
6. W. James Fowler, *Stages of Faith* (New York: Harper Collins, 1981).
7. Maureen O'Hara, "Person-Centered Approach as Conscientizacao," *Journal of Humanistic Psychology* 29, no. 1 (January 1989): 11–35, https://doi.org/10.1177/0022167889291002.
8. DeGruy Leary, *Post-Traumatic Slave Syndrome*; Paulo Freire, *Pedagogy of the Oppressed* (Harmondsworth, Middlesex: Penguin Education, 1972).
9. Stacey Patton, *Spare the Kids: Why Whupping Children Won't Save Black America* (Boston: Beacon, 2017).

References

Akinyela, Makungu M. "Conscious Parenting Family Circles: An African-Centered Critical Pedagogy." *Cultural Studies, Critical Methodologies* 6, no. 1 (2006): 155–65. https://doi.org/10.1177/1532708605282812.
Fowler, James W. *Stages of Faith: The Psychology of Human Development and the Quest for Meaning.* San Francisco: Harper & Row, 1981.
Freire, Paulo. *Pedagogy of the Oppressed.* Translated by Myra Bergman Ramos. 50th anniversary ed. New York: Bloomsbury Academic, 2018.

Kirylo, James D., and James H. Cone. "Paulo Freire, Black Theology of Liberation, and Liberation Theology: A Conversation with James H. Cone." *Counterpoints* 385 (2011): 195–212. http://www.jstor.org/stable/42980930.

Maslow, Abraham H. *Toward a Psychology of Being*. New York: Van Nostrand, 1968.

O'Hara, Maureen. "Person-Centered Approach as Conscientizacao: The Works of Carl Rogers and Paulo Freire." *Journal of Humanistic Psychology* 29, no. 1 (1989): 11–35. https://doi.org/10.1177/0022167889291002.

Patton, Stacey. *Spare the Kids: Why Whupping Children Won't Save Black America*. Boston: Beacon, 2017.

Williams, Yolanda. https://parentingdecolonized.com/.

14

Reflective Practice for Sexual Formation

MARGARET CONLEY

While having conversations about faith formation and sexuality with children, young adults, and other adults may be uncomfortable for some people, doing so is nevertheless important. Though we church folks often struggle to admit it, we are inherently sexual beings. We are oriented toward connection, and sexuality is a part of the way that happens. Understanding our lives from a physical, emotional, social, and spiritual need for sexuality is vital to the creation of healthy lives and healthy behaviors in our church spaces. While sexuality is an essential topic for all of us, it is crucial for us to explore the messages we send about what sexuality should look like and the potential harm that can come from narrow models of what healthy sexuality can look like.

Ultimately, we want to build a positive sense of connection among all members of our faith communities so that we can help connect all to the Divine. It is important to say that sex and sexuality are difficult for churches for many reasons that we do not have time to review here. Because many of us are uncomfortable thinking about and talking about sex, it will take work for us to have these conversations in fruitful ways. Reflective practice can be a tool for helping us address these conversations in healthy and expansive ways. Reflective practice is consciously thinking about and analyzing one's own experiences, actions, and decisions to gain insight and function more effectively in the future. This practice is an indispensable tool for including sexuality as a part of our faith formation practices. In other words, the invitation here is to ask ourselves questions like: What do I believe about sex? Do I acknowledge and own my own sexuality? Do I have beliefs about certain sexual expressions or orientations being connected to sin?

Sexuality is a part of our human experience and is a part of God's design for human beings. So, as we teach about God's intentions for humanity, we have opportunities to include healthy sexuality as a part of that. Many churches, in efforts to curb what have been seen as sinful sexual actions, have given laundry lists of things not to do but have not provided guidelines for what healthy sexuality can look like. While this can create painful points of shame for all of us, it can be especially detrimental to people who hold a sexually minoritized identity, such as lesbian, gay, bisexual, transgender, queer, intersex, asexual, or another such identity (LGBTQIA+). Churches can attend to children (and adults) as holistic beings by building the skills for helping children understand their sexuality and having open conversations in churches about it.

In Matthew 19, Jesus covers topics that span the wide range of human existence, from sex to marriage to divorce. Following this model, churches also must be willing to have tough conversations and not allow topics that we perceive as taboo to keep us from honoring the lived experience of community members. Having these conversations is especially crucial for sexuality because many LGBTQIA+ folks feel shunned or left out of the Christian community, and still others have not had opportunities to understand sexuality in a healthy way. Because we are all made in the image of God, that totality of our humanness deserves respect and attention. To love the God in each of us is to love all of us, to acknowledge that each of us is God's good creation. Our sexual expression is simply one way that good creation can be displayed.

Necessary Conversations

When we talk with children, youth, and or young adults about sexuality, we tend to focus on purely physical acts, and typically those which we deem should not be performed. However, this strategy does not help people understand healthy ways to engage their sexuality. A consequence is that many of us have been taught to deny our sexuality, which can complicate our romantic relationships and confuse our understanding of our own bodies. When we apply the strategy of reflective practice to early sexual education, we invite ourselves and young people into a process of discerning what healthy sexuality looks like. We engage the doctrines of our faith tradition with our own sense of morality and a healthy, realistic understanding of sexual functioning. For instance, when we acknowledge that sexual desire is a real and present part of our lives, we are more equipped to have healthy conversations about consent and to negotiate boundaries for all forms of physical touch and connection. Allowing for critical thinking and reflection helps us to build skills for healthy decision-making around sex without feeling a need to indoctrinate children with beliefs that have been passed down among adults.[1]

Talking about sexuality with young people also builds skills for all of us to understand ourselves more fully and to understand how we use our faith to make sense of ourselves and the world. We as adults have the opportunity to understand our own bodies and to name the expansiveness of creation in the diversity of ways God has created us to understand and connect to our bodies and with one another. In other words, when we as adults begin to reflect on our own bodies and sexuality, we provide a model for youth and young adults to do the same.[2] Our process is less about transmitting a set of rules and more about engaging in critical thinking about how God allows us to understand ourselves and relate to one another.³ We often treat youth as if they are too young for particular conversations, but part of raising faithful children is reminding them of the importance of their big questions and holding space for them to explore them safely. This helps to create a sense of autonomy and curiosity that can sustain their faith journeys far into adulthood. Denying them an opportunity to wrestle with these issues can do harm, for children might often be left with the message that their sexuality is somehow sinful or not of God. Sex and sexuality are not merely a physical act, but sexuality is a part of how we understand our bodies and ourselves.

Faith Formation and Sexuality

Faith formation can be influenced by various factors, including religious teachings, personal experiences, and interactions with a faith community. Faith formation is an invitation to develop a critical conscience; this conscience can influence one's understanding and interpretation of religious teachings, and one's faith can shape their moral values and decision-making. A person with a critical conscience may question certain aspects of their faith tradition, challenge religious teachings that conflict with their moral values, and seek a deeper understanding and interpretation of their religious beliefs. According to the work of theologian James Fowler, this questioning and critiquing of the faith is seen as an advanced form of faith development.

Fowler's stages of faith are built through the lens of Jean Piaget's stages of cognitive development, Lawrence Kohlberg's stages of moral development, and Erik Erikson's stages of development. All three of these theories of development are held as part of a gold standard that can be used to understand the naturally unfolding development of human beings over their lifespan. Just as these theories involve cognitive, moral, and relational development in human beings, our discussions of human sexuality tap into all these domains in the context of our faith. As children grow and develop, their experience of faith can become more complex over time—they have questions about how to navigate the normal experiences of their lives—desire, relationship, conflict, and sexuality through the lens of their faith. Dr. Benjamin Jones reimagined Fowler's work to include four stages: religious socialization, early questioning, exploration and engagement, and refinement. In this reworking, we still see that challenge, questioning, and personalization are key components to spiritual maturation.[4]

Jones's inclusion of challenge, questioning, and personalization is useful as we explore how to have meaningful conversations about faith and sexuality. Reflective practice allows us to hold the truth that all of us are in a constant state of evolving and changing. We are allowed to seek new understandings about ourselves and God. We are allowed to change our minds. We are allowed to work to understand our bodies and our own sense of sexuality in new and different ways. Our goal is not just to deposit things into people as a part of faith formation but to share the tools that support long-term growth and development.[5] Just like sexuality, faith development is highly individual, and the timing and progression through these stages can vary from person to person. Reflective practice opens the door for healthy faith development and open discussion around sexual orientation while respecting individuality. Our faith helps us to understand what God says about us and how to treat one another, and we can each build an individual understanding of what it means to honor God with our bodies and in our sexual expression.

The Basics: Terminology about Sexuality

As discussed earlier, many churches have focused our conversations related to sex around what not to do instead of outlining what healthy human sexuality looks like. As a consequence, many of us may not even have the language to talk about sex in healthy ways. This section provides some basic terms to get these conversations started. Sexual orientation refers to an individual's enduring pattern of emotional, romantic, and/or sexual attraction to individuals. Sexuality is fluid, meaning a person's understanding of sexuality changes throughout their lifespan. In our society, we make assumptions that people have a heterosexual orientation, meaning they are attracted only to people of the opposite sex. Many Christian traditions have explicit teachings about heterosexuality being the only valid sexual orientation. These norms can make it difficult for people who do not have this sexual orientation to feel included in faith communities and even to feel that they have access to the love of God. By expanding our conversations about sexual orientation, we provide space for people to see and understand themselves fully, both as children of God and as members of our communities.

Sexual orientation includes three dimensions: "attraction, behavior, and identity."[6] Sexual attraction refers to an individual's emotional, romantic, or sexual desire toward other people. It is the subjective experience of being drawn to someone in a sexual or romantic way. Sexual attraction can be directed toward individuals of the same gender (homosexual attraction), opposite gender (heterosexual attraction), or both genders (bisexual attraction). It is important to note that sexual attraction exists on a spectrum, and individuals may experience varying degrees or types of attraction.[7]

Sexual behavior refers to the actions or activities that individuals engage in to express their sexual desires or fulfill their sexual needs. It encompasses a wide range of activities, including but not limited to sexual intercourse, kissing, touching, masturbation, oral sex, and various forms of sexual play. Sexual behavior is highly personal and can differ greatly between individuals based on their preferences, values, cultural norms, and consent.[8]

Sexual identity refers to an individual's internal sense of their own sexual orientation or gender identity. It is how individuals understand and define themselves in terms of their sexual attractions, desires, and relationships. Sexual identity can include labels such as heterosexual, homosexual, bisexual, pansexual, asexual, or queer, among others. It is a deeply personal and subjective aspect of a person's self-identity and can evolve or change over time as individuals explore and understand their own feelings and experiences.[9]

Many of us have not had these conversations in churches. However, understanding ourselves in this way is crucially important for us to have healthy and fulfilling relationships. Essentially, the opportunity is to ask ourselves: How did God create me? How do I understand myself? How do I share myself with others?

We have an intuitive understanding that during puberty, adolescents begin to feel and express desire in recognizable ways. But puberty is not the beginning of our status as sexual beings; according to theorists Morton and Barbara Kelsey, sexual orientation is "a part of our basic personality pattern and should be understood from a psychological and physiological context."[10] Thus, sexual orientation should be seen as an inherent and deeply ingrained aspect of a person's identity. Sexual orientation is typically experienced as a fundamental and unchangeable part of who we are. Sexual orientation exists on a continuum, with individuals experiencing a range of attractions and identities.[11] This research provides us with two important truths: first, we cannot conform or change a person's sexuality to fit what we believe is right, and second, sexual identities may not fit into neatly divided boxes. The use of reflective practice helps us to meet people where they are and gives all of us the autonomy to envision the particularities of how God created us.

The challenge for faith communities is to provide opportunities for individuals to define and name their orientation for themselves rather than the community ascribing assumed (and sometimes incorrect) labels. For faith communities to do this well, we must commit to loving a person as they would like to be loved. Our call is to accept people as they are and to honor the fullness of how they show up to us, including sexual orientation. We can also commit to understanding and learning about the person. Learning how to address and be present with the individual, respecting their personhood (for example, using their correct pronouns) and understanding how they identify is vital to the faith formation of the individual and the community in which the individual resides.

Reflective practice requires us to build comfort with our own bodies and embodiment. Many faith communities have taught us to "get out of the flesh" and "get into the spirit," yet our spirit is housed within our bodies. Our aversion to "flesh" can lead us to demonize the very natural experiences that are a part of our humanness. We can become comfortable with our bodies by becoming aware of the emotions, reactions, and physical sensations on a regular basis. Reflective practice and embodiment complement one another. Sitting with ourselves, mind and body, helps us to enhance self-awareness, promote personal growth, and navigate our human experiences in a healthy way.[12] For example, knowing what physical sensations are associated with sadness, pleasure, or anger helps us to know ourselves better. Understanding these feelings can, in turn, help us to understand our sexuality more deeply and fully by identifying what brings us pleasure and what we do not like, building the capacity to communicate.

We must know our bodies, be connected to our bodies, and have an emotional understanding of our bodies for healthy reflective practice to happen between adults and children, and among adults. Adults have great power; how we see ourselves is how children will begin to see themselves. Much like the disciples attempted to dismiss the children present when Jesus was teaching, many adults may dismiss or belittle the experiences and perspectives of children rather than help them understand themselves better. This sends an unspoken message about their worthiness (or lack thereof) that children can carry for years to come. The goal is to see children and have children see themselves as full members of the faith community, just as Jesus did.

The Effects of Dismissal and Understanding of the Self[13]

I have been working to make the case that churches have an opportunity to take the lead in educating children about sex, sexuality, and healthy ways to engage in relationships. As adults, reflective practice will allow us to explore and examine both our beliefs and what we have been taught about sex and sexuality. However, we can only do this successfully if we are truly willing to reflect on ourselves. Reflective practice works only if one can see themselves with compassion and allow that to be shared with others. In most westernized religious environments, reflective practice has been ascribed to the understanding of the sacred text, often the Bible; however, I suggest that we must see ourselves as the sacred text being read by others. Our actions become a pathway through which people experience God and the world.

As the Pauline letters offer, we are living letters (2 Corinthians 3:2-3). In westernized culture, we have been made to believe that something is wrong with us, and God had to bring something to us for us to be saved from ourselves. These frames can often lead to feelings of shame and condemnation of ourselves, founded in a belief that we cannot trust our own desires or feelings. With the use of this language, we dismiss our story and our personhood; we forgo "a steady beat" of inner harmony and decline to know ourselves deeply and live into the fullness of who we are. When we dismiss our personhood, we make it harder to accept, honor, and celebrate natural and healthy expressions of sexuality.

Psychologist Na'im Akbar offers that if we can get to know ourselves internally, we can become more connected to how our emotions work, paying attention to how our bodies and minds are responding.[14] This helps us to understand our relationships with God and others, our sense of embodiment, and our sexuality. When adults can do this for themselves, we invite children to do the same. Making conversations regarding sexual orientation available for children earlier in their development may allow children to be more attuned with who they are and how they see the Divine versus attempting to live into indoctrination that is experienced as oppressive for many. Our challenge as adults is to convene these conversations with a deep self-understanding and without an agenda.

Using the Power of Play as a Tool

Reflective practice allows us to explore and understand ourselves as we guide children in their own self-understanding. We are allowed to give narratives for our own beliefs and values while also respecting the diversity of beliefs that children bring. We can see the intentions we may have toward working with children. We are also able to learn from children during our engagement with them, which allows adults to remain in a state of perpetual growth. It helps us create inclusive and open spaces for children to explore their spirituality and sexuality and to develop a strong foundation of faith in autonomy, guided by the wisdom of the faith community. Regarding sexual orientation, reflective practice enables us to examine our own biases, assumptions, and attitudes toward diverse sexual orientations.[15] A part of this process is to say that churches have not always been safe spaces for LGBTQIA+ folks. Humility helps us approach this topic with sensitivity, respect, and acceptance, ensuring that children feel safe and supported in their journey of self-discovery and understanding.

Reflective practice also encourages us to be aware of developmental needs and age-appropriate information for children. It prompts us to seek creative ways to engage children in conversations, activities, and experiences that foster their understanding, empathy, and self-acceptance. Ultimately, the goal of reflective practice is to ensure that we are providing a supportive and nurturing environment for children to explore and develop their faith and understanding of sexuality. This goal can be met through the power of play.

The "powers of play" promoted by Schaefer and Drewes can be used in reflective practice for faith formation and can be a component of the universalizing formation of faith regarding sexual orientation for the faith community.[16] Though often conceptualized for children, play can be a benefit to all. It allows us to let down our defenses and engage in deep levels of connection to ourselves and others. The four outcomes of the powers of play are facilitating communication, fostering emotional wellness, enhancing social relationships, and increasing personal strengths.[17]

Facilitating Communication

Play can facilitate communication so that people at multiple levels of maturity can understand. Ways to facilitate communication include things like self-expression and teaching. Self-expression provides a brave space for one to share their thoughts, feelings, and beliefs about sexual orientation. Encouraging self-expression allows adults and children to reflect on their own identity, values, and faith in a supportive and nonjudgmental environment.

When people feel free to express themselves, we make space for curiosity and creativity. With creativity, both adults and children can work through different scenarios, roles, and perspectives, helping them gain a deeper understanding of diverse experiences. Talking through curiosity regarding sexual orientation and its connection to our faith leaves the pathways to communication open and makes ways for continued for both adults and children. Role-playing scenarios related to consent and boundaries can help to increase confidence and autonomy in navigating relationships.

Teaching age-appropriate information is also important in facilitating communication. When we provide children with age-appropriate information about sexuality, such as the appropriate language for genitalia or normalizing sexual desire or attraction, we can tailor the content to their developmental stage and use language they can understand. We should be mindful of their maturity level and address their questions without overwhelming them. Play becomes the tool we use to have challenging conversations while providing concrete and accessible examples.

Fostering Emotional Wellness

Play fosters emotional wellness and is a healthy way to manage stress. Fostering emotional wellness includes opening pathways to healthier emotional responses; this is especially relevant when discussing sexuality, as it can bring up challenging and sometimes distressing emotions in faith communities. As we work through reflective practice, we need to use our emotions as information about how we understand our sexuality. For instance, if I become anxious or angry when discussing sexuality, what can I begin to learn about my own understanding of my sexual identity or attraction? This exploration helps our work around sexuality to become understandable, digestible, and empowering. Role-modeling fosters a brave space for emotional wellness. It demonstrates a healthy relationship with yourself, respect for yourself, and acceptance of yourself. Play helps to decrease the emotional intensity of these conversations, which can overwhelm and bring up issues of shame and confusion. By identifying these emotions we can learn to reckon with them. Showing compassion, empathy, and understanding when working through this topic helps create positive feelings, making the space more comfortable for future reflection and growth.

Enhancing Social Relationships

Play enhances healthy, positive relationships between adults and children by changing the power dynamic. In playful encounters, children can state their understanding of faith, act as experts, and be on level ground with adults; this opens the door for communication and connection.

Enhancing social relationships can also allow for trust, emotional regulation, and attunement (emotional matching) to have challenging conversations. These relationships help to neutralize the trauma many of us have experienced related to sex and sexuality in the church. In this context, different perspectives can be shared, discussed, and understood. For example, you might consider playing a trivia game related to human sexual development to share information while building camaraderie among those playing.

Increasing Personal Strengths

Play offers creative ways to increase personal strengths. Personal strengths include solving problems, enhancing moral and psychological development and resiliency, and promoting self-regulation and self-esteem. Through play, adults and children can begin to think critically about a shared understanding of faith formation and sexuality.

By engaging in critical thinking activities related to sexuality and faith, we can cocreate a brave space for questioning stereotypes, challenging biases, and developing a more nuanced understanding of sex and sexuality. Play allows these processes to happen with less fear of judgment or rebuke. This nonthreatening environment supports a deeper understanding of beliefs and connection to what is believed and openness to further engage in future dialogue around the subject.

Churches can and should take an active stance in teaching children about consent, bodily autonomy, and the importance of healthy boundaries in relationships. When we engage using reflective practice and critical thinking, we allow members of our community to develop agency and empowerment related to their sexuality. This is a pathway to help children understand the moral and ethical aspects of sexuality within their faith while also promoting acceptance and respect for others who may hold different beliefs. Agency opens the door for discussion on consent and boundaries. It also promotes positive body image, fostering self-acceptance and self-love. This is powerful because it opens the door to listening, learning, and loving with and through authentic beliefs and not indoctrinated systems of unholy care and concern.

Further Considerations and Conclusions

Reflective practice is a valuable approach to faith formation and discussions of sexuality. It requires that those who are modeling faith formation to seek healing for themselves to enhance their ability to support children's development in these areas of sexuality and faith formation overall. Using play as a modality, congregations can begin to foster low-intensity conversations that help children and adults alike to understand their sexuality and develop a personal moral understanding of appropriate sexual behaviors. Due to the possibility of traumatic and harmful experiences in the past, these conversations need to be holistic and ongoing, to create a new ethic around sex and sexuality in the church.

For parents and caregivers who would like materials with which to engage in reflective places around sexuality, we offer the following resources.

UCC OUR WHOLE LIVES RESOURCE PAGE
   https://www.uccresources.com/products/our-whole-lives-owl-curriculum?_pos=1&_sid=d6f4d95c5&_ss=r&variant=39779890593855&variant=39779890593855.
   Our Whole Lives: Parent Guide, 2nd ed. This guide is designed to help parents (and other loving caretakers) respond to children's questions and concerns about sexuality. Used for both the K–1 and 4–6 OWL resources.
   "Parents and Caregivers as Sexuality Educators" (free PDF download). A resource for parents and caregivers to explore their roles as primary sexuality educators of their children. Written with UCC prayer, Scripture, and reflection pieces, this small group ministry format resource

can be used with parents and caregivers of any age, children or teens, and is customizable to your group's particular interest. Access the free download from this site.

ONLINE RESOURCES
Jen Hatmaker. https://jenhatmaker.com/me-course/parenting-lgbtqia/
Reframing Our Stories. https://www.reframingourstories.com/about

PLANNED PARENTHOOD CHRISTIAN RESOURCE
https://www.plannedparenthood.org/files/8114/0042/5971/CFL_Guide_web.pdf

BOOKS
Cindy Wong Brandt's book *Parenting Forward* is about more than sexuality, but it also addresses sexuality: https://cindywangbrandt.com/parenting-forward/. Study guide can be downloaded from the site.

These Are Our Bodies Foundation Book: Talking Faith and Sexuality at Church and Home (Episcopal Church): https://www.churchpublishing.org/theseareourbodiesfoundation

RESOURCES FROM KATE OTT AND LORIEN CARTER
Creating a Sexual Ethic (video and lesson plan). https://yaleyouthministryinstitute.org/resource/creating-a-sexual-ethic/

Sex + Faith: Talking with Your Child from Birth to Adolescence. https://www.thethoughtfulchristian.com/Products/0664237991/sex--faith.aspx

Sex, Tech, and Faith: Ethics for a Digital Age (youth guide included). https://www.eerdmans.com/9780802878465/

"Talking about Gender and Sexuality with Youth." Dr. Kate Ott. https://www.youtube.com/playlist?list=PLd8AZSL0LG2Nt8SihWge478ZPJOffZSne

Kate Ott and Lorien Carter. "ReVisioning Sexuality: Relational Joy and Embodied Flourishing." *Journal of Youth and Theology*, March 25, 2021. https://yaleyouthministryinstitute.org/resource/revisioning-sexuality-relational-joy-and-embodied-flourishing/

YALE YOUTH MINISTRY INSTITUTE
(VIDEOS AND LESSON PLAN)
Being a Welcome and Inclusive Youth Group. https://yaleyouthministryinstitute.org/resource/being-a-welcome-and-inclusive-youth-group/
Ministry to LGBTQ+ Youth. https://yaleyouthministryinstitute.org/resources/topics/trending-topics/ministry-with-lgbtq-youth/

Questions for Discussion

1. What opportunities does your faith community offer for conversations and/or resources about sexuality?
2. What resources do you need for reflective practices about sexuality and faith formation?

Notes

1. Brian E. Neubauer et al., "How Phenomenology Can Help Us Learn from the Experiences of Others," *Perspectives on Medical Education* 8, no. 2 (April 5, 2019): 90–97, https://doi.org/10.1007/s40037-019-0509-2.
2. Lisa Sowle Cahill, *Sex, Gender, and Christian Ethics* (Cambridge University Press, 1996), 22.
3. Cahill, *Sex, Gender, and Christian Ethics*, 23.
4. Benjamin Jones, "Reimagining Fowler's Stages of Faith: Shifting from a Seven Stage to a Four Step Framework for Faith Development," *Journal of Beliefs & Values* 44 (March 9, 2022): 160.
5. Paulo Freire, "The Banking Concept of Education," in *Thinking about Schools*, ed. Eleanor Blair Hilty (New York: Routledge, 2018), 117.
6. Andrew Park, Beyond the Binary: A Guidance for Inclusion of LGBTI People in Development Activities, CanWaCH (Canadian Partnership for Women and Children), Resource Centre, June 9, 2021, https://canwach.ca/learning/beyond-the-binary-a-guidance-for-inclusion-of-lgbti-people-in-development-activities.
7. Park, Beyond the Binary.
8. Park, Beyond the Binary.
9. Park, Beyond the Binary.

10. Morton Kelsey and Barbara Kelsey, "Homosexualities," in *Homosexuality and Christian Faith: Questions of Conscience for the Churches*, ed. Henry Wink (Minneapolis: Fortress, 1999), 63.
11. Kelsey and Kelsey, "Homosexualities," 71.
12. Barbara Sprung, Marshal Miller, and Sam Allen, "Our Whole Lives: Lifespan Sexuality Education," Unitarian Universalist Association, August 31, 2022, https://www.uua.org/re/owl.
13. Na'im Akbar, *The Community of Self* (Tallahassee, FL: Mind Productions & Associates, 2002); Leonard L. Riskin, "Managing Inner and Outer Conflict: Selves, Subpersonalities, and Internal Family Systems," *18 Harvard Negotiation Law Review* 18 (2013): 1–69, https://ssrn.com/abstract=2390872.
14. Na'im Akbar, *The Community of Self*.
15. Hesook Suzie Kim, "Critical Reflective Inquiry for Knowledge Development in Nursing Practice," *Journal of Advanced Nursing* 29, no. 5 (May 1999): 1205–12.
16. Charles E. Schaefer and Athena A. Drewes, *The Therapeutic Powers of Play: 20 Core Agents of Change* (Hoboken, NJ: Wiley, 2014).
17. Schaefer and Drewes, *The Therapeutic Powers of Play*.

References

Akbar, Na'im. *The Community of Self*. Tallahassee, FL: Mind Productions & Associates, 2002.
Andresen, Josefine B., Christian Graugaard, Mikael Andersson, Mikkel K. Bahnsen, and Morten Frisch. "Childhood Gender Non-conformity, Sexual Orientation, and Mental Health Problems among 18- to 89-Year-Old Danes." *World Psychiatry* 22, no. 2 (June 2023): 334–35. https://doi.org/10.1002/wps.21096. PMID: 37159358; PMCID: PMC10168161.
Cahill, Lisa Sowle. *Sex, Gender, and Christian Ethics*. Cambridge: Cambridge University Press, 1996.
Freire, Paulo. "The Banking Concept of Education," in Hilty, Eleanor Blair, ed., *Thinking about Schools*. New York: Routledge, 2018.
―――. *Pedagogy of the Oppressed*. Translated by Myra Bergman Ramos. 50th anniversary ed. New York: Bloomsbury Academic, 2018.
Fowler, James W., and Robin W. Levin. "Stages of Faith: The Psychology of Human Development and the Quest for Meaning." *Review of Religious Research* 25, no. 1 (1983): 77.
Honest, Barbara Sprung, Marshall Miller, and Sam Allen. "Our Whole Lives: Lifespan Sexuality Education." Unitarian Universalist Association. August 31, 2022. https://www.uua.org/re/owl.
Jones, Benjamin. "Reimagining Fowler's Stages of Faith: Shifting from a Seven Stage to a Four Step Framework for Faith Development." *Journal of Beliefs & Values* 44 (2022): 159–72.
Kelsey, Morton, and Barbara Kelsey. "Homosexualities." In Kelsey and Kelsey, *Homosexuality and Christian Faith: Questions of Conscience for the Churches*, edited by Henry Wink, 63–76. Minneapolis: Fortress, 1999.
Kim, Hesook Suzie. "Critical Reflective Inquiry for Knowledge Development in Nursing Practice." *Journal of Advanced Nursing* 29, no. 5 (May 1999): 1205–12. https://doi.org/10.1046/j.1365-2648.1999.01005.x. PMID: 10320505.
Leonard L. Riskin. "Managing Inner and Outer Conflict: Selves, Subpersonalities, and Internal Family Systems." *Harvard Negotiation Law Review* 18 (2013): 1–69. https://ssrn.com/abstract=2390872.

Neubauer, Brian E., Catherine T. Witkop, and Lara Varpio. "How Phenomenology Can Help Us Learn from the Experiences of Others." *Perspectives on Medical Education* 8, no. 2 (April 5, 2019): 90–97. https://doi.org/10.1007/s40037-019-0509-2.

Park, Andrew. Beyond the Binary: A Guidance for Inclusion of LGBTI People in Development Activities. CanWaCH (Canadian Partnership for Women and Children). Resource Centre. June 9, 2021. https://canwach.ca/learning/beyond-the-binary-a-guidance-for-inclusion-of-lgbti-people-in-development-activities.

Schaefer, Charles E., and Athena A. Drewes. *The Therapeutic Powers of Play: 20 Core Agents of Change*. Hoboken, NJ: Wiley, 2014.

Schwartz, Richard C., and Martha Sweezy. *Internal Family Systems Therapy*. 2nd ed. New York: Guilford, 2019.

15

All Children Are a Part of the Village: Neurodivergence in Communities of Faith

TIMOTHY LUCAS

It Takes a Village

It takes a village to raise a child. —*African Proverb*

Growing in faith does not happen automatically but requires personal commitment. Scripture encourages us to love God with all our hearts and to love our neighbors as we love ourselves. These statements imply that there are actionable things we can do to fulfill these commandments. We must be intentional in our effort to learn strategies to help us deepen our faith, develop a stronger relationship with God, and strengthen our relationships with one another. Without encouragement, mentorship, and support, growing deeper in faith can be daunting for adults and even more difficult for children and adolescents. Now, imagine being an autistic child trying to understand the complexities of what "growing deeper in faith" means. Should the sole responsibility for these children's spiritual development be on the parent or caregiver? How can congregations and communities of faith support families with an autistic child to help them grow deeper in their faith?

Scripture suggests that parents are responsible for teaching foundational biblical truths to their children; however, having raised four children myself, I do not think God's intent was for them to do it alone. As the parent of an autistic child, I can testify that this is especially true for raising an autistic child. I believe congregations and communities of faith can be key supports in assisting parents and caregivers in children's faith development. I am not implying that children cannot grow deeper in faith if they are not engaged in traditional church activities or that parents cannot develop solid faith foundations in their children. In the words of the age-old African proverb, "It takes a village to raise a child." Congregations can augment parents in helping children grow deeper in their faith by creating spaces and opportunities conducive to spiritual growth, especially for neurodivergent children. Understanding the characteristics of an autistic child could be a starting point for congregations trying to assist. To help support this theory, I will use the below fictitious case study to extract learning points to develop strategies to help children with processing differences grow in their faith.

Katie's Traumatic Day

After returning from one of the most traumatic experiences she had encountered in a while, Katie hastily walked into her house and went straight to her room. She put on her headphones, selected her favorite playlist, and zoned out for hours. She needed time to unwind from the events of the day. Her mother did not understand why Katie was so upset and tried to communicate with her. "Katie, did you enjoy the church service? The people were very nice," her mother said excitedly. "It was terrible," Katie sobbed. "I never want to go back there!" So, what could have caused Katie to feel this way about her experience at church? How could her response have been so different from her mother's? Let's rewind and tell you what happened.

Earlier that morning, Katie was awakened by her mother telling her to hurry and get dressed because they were visiting a new church. Disoriented, Katie quickly showered, dressed, and headed downstairs for breakfast. Because they were running late, her mother said they would stop by a drive-through restaurant on the way to church instead of making Katie's favorite pancakes for breakfast. They managed to get to church a few minutes before the service started. As first-time guests, they were greeted with hugs from the ushers, who gave them church bulletins with the order of service and then escorted them to the front row of the church designated for visitors. The senior pastor was running late, so the service was delayed for fifteen minutes while loud music played in the background. During this waiting period, random congregational members came to the front to greet Katie and her mother to welcome them and thank them for visiting their church.

The service eventually started with high-energy song selections from the praise band. Katie did not know the words to songs the worship team was singing but tried following the lyrics on the massive monitor behind the main stage. At one point in the service, guests were invited to stand up and introduce themselves to the congregation. Embarrassed that all eyes were on her, Katie reluctantly stood up as her mother introduced them. Afterward people seemed to come from everywhere, greeting them, giving them hugs, shaking their hands, and doing their best to make Katie and her mother feel welcome. The service continued with more singing, dancing, and a thirty-minute sermon from the senior pastor. Katie tried to understand the sermon but was distracted by a constant humming noise from the sound system. Following the service, Katie and her mother were escorted by an usher into a room where other first-time guests were gathered to meet the senior pastor. They chatted for a few minutes, then Katie and her mother left to return home.

You may be asking, "What is the matter with Katie? It seems the church was inviting, engaging, and friendly." The issue is that Katie is ten years old, autistic, and an extreme introvert. Being neurodivergent, her brain processes information differently from that of others. While this church seemed intentional about making guests feel welcome, they unintentionally created a traumatic experience for Katie.

While the various elements of Katie's story may seem ordinary, several aspects of this experience can be overwhelming and traumatic for children with processing differences. As an autistic child, Katie experiences life differently. Although neurodivergent individuals vary, some of the characteristics of Katie's functioning include challenges with social communication (little eye contact), sensitivity to light and sound, speech and language challenges, repetitive behaviors (does not easily adapt to change), and hyperfocus on specific interests. Understanding these characteristics common among neurodivergent individuals helps us to see why several actions in Katie's story can be problematic for children like her. The good news is that we can use elements of this story to present ideas of how congregations can help children like Katie grow in their faith without being traumatized by their church experiences. Let's start by identifying common characteristics of neurodivergent children.

What Is Neurodivergence?

Neurodivergence is "individual differences in brain functioning regarded as normal variations within the human population."[1] Common conditions of neurodivergent individuals include attention deficit hyperactivity disorder (ADHD), dyslexia, dyspraxia, or Tourette syndrome. Another neurodivergent diagnosis that has garnered attention over the past few years is autism spectrum disorder (ASD). ASD is "a neurodevelopmental disorder characterized by markedly impaired social interactions and verbal and nonverbal communication; narrow interests; and repetitive behavior."[2] For some neurodivergent individuals, additional characteristics may include, as the APA Dictionary of Psychology describes, "difficulties with social-emotional reciprocity, abnormal social approach, and difficulty with back-and-forth conversations."[3] Some children who are neurodivergent experience unique life challenges that require intervention and support to help them engage in the community. With some notable exceptions, there are limited resources explicitly addressing the needs of neurodivergent individuals in churches and faith-based communities.

Think about your church's various ministries and programs. Are there programs in place intentionally designed to minister to autistic individuals? Despite the unique social, emotional, and mental challenges neurodivergent children face daily, faith communities often neglect them, and the parents or caregivers are left alone to assist the children in developing their faith. Not only will addressing this issue benefit the autistic child, but it will also help the parents and caregivers. This is a critically important opportunity for congregations and communities of faith to provide a desperately needed service.

How Can We Help?

Let's revisit Katie's story and provide strategies that congregations and communities of faith can use to help children like Katie grow deeper in their faith. It will help us to break down the worship experience activity, symptoms of Katie's particular neurodivergence, and the results that were contributing factors in making it a traumatic day for her. First, the ushers' and greeters' welcomes were difficult for Katie because her anxiety often has her avoiding eye contact. Fellowship with strangers, given her limited communication skills, evoked feelings of isolation and depression. While the shifts in worship timing and patterns may have been interpreted by some as authentic and spontaneous, these changes brought additional anxiety for Katie. Worship starting late triggered Katie's rather rigid personal rules and routines, amplifying her anxiety. And while it might have gone unnoticed by many people, the hum in the sound system caused additional discomfort, given Katie's sensitivity to sound and light. Not everyone with autism would have these same responses, but this is what Katie experienced. And her reactions were probably misunderstood by the well-intentioned people who went out of their way to be welcoming by their own standards.

Being aware of the challenges that neurodivergent children face daily could help congregations and communities of faith be more attentive to their needs and develop programs and strategies to accommodate them. In her book *Autism and Your Church,* Barbara Newman listed ten strategies that congregations and faith communities could use to be more purposeful and intentional when ministering to neurodivergent children.[4] Two strategies that could be easily implemented include gathering some general information about neurodivergence and sharing that information with others who need to know (i.e., youth workers, teachers, ushers/greeters, etc.). Reliable websites to get information include the Center for Disease Control (www.cdc.gov), the American Academy of Child and Adolescent Psychiatry (www.aacap.org), and the Interagency Autism Coordinating Committee (www.iacc.hhs.gov). Speaking with family members and caregivers of autistic children to gain firsthand knowledge of their challenges and hearing their testimonies and success stories would also be helpful for church leaders. Understanding the needs and abilities of neurodivergent children can benefit everyone involved, including the child, the youth worker, and the parents and caregivers.

In many churches, the worship experience may involve personal interactions that some neurotypical individuals may welcome and even come to expect.[5] A greeting in the parking lot, hugs in the sanctuary, "touch your neighbor" moments, preacher "call and response" sermons, and fellowship dinners are standard practices across various church denominations. This type of social activity can be traumatic for an autistic child (and even for many neurotypical individuals).

The church is an institution where personal relationships are fundamental to helping people grow spiritually and develop a deeper faith. The social aspect of congregational life can unintentionally leave an autistic child on the fringes due to their inability to properly respond when greeted or to engage in conversation. Additionally, differences in social skills make it difficult to make friends or engage in social events that involve group activities with other children. Additionally, communication in social settings like church gatherings is known for sharing personal information (i.e., testimonies), which requires the hearer to provide acknowledgment, verbal feedback, and moral support. Some autistic individuals experience "persistent deficits in social communication and social interaction."[6] Their differences in social-emotional reciprocity manifest in their difficulty in responding appropriately to others' emotions, which is one reason they have problems making friends or feeling like they belong in specific social settings. In addition, some autistic individuals do not correctly process social cues like gestures and facial expressions, making it challenging to engage in conversations with neurotypical people.

While characteristics may be present throughout life, neurodivergent individuals can learn strategies to improve social-emotional reciprocity skills with training and intervention. A study by the Koegel Autism Center concluded that "video feedback intervention" helped improve participants' verbal expression during empathetic conversations. This skill is vital to creating and maintaining relationships. Additional research investigated the "effectiveness of social skills interventions." It concluded that the social functioning of persons with autism could be improved, reducing loneliness and potentially alleviating co-morbid psychiatric symptoms.[7] Communities of faith may have congregants who can assist in allowing space and patience to practice social skills to strengthen the social-emotional communication skills of neurodivergent children. This could allow them to participate in communal activities, experience a sense of belonging, and feel a part of the community. Youth workers and teachers are encouraged to engage in conversation with the parents or caregivers of an autistic child to understand better their strengths, gifts, and areas of interest. Additional preparation could include conversations with professional behavioral health specialists and special education teachers to help the youth worker create the most productive environment for the child.

Opportunities

Unfortunately, Katie's fictional story is a reality for thousands of children. However, churches and faith communities can take steps to assist neurodivergent children. Below are several opportunities congregations and communities of faith can incorporate into their church programming to help neurodivergent children grow deeper in their faith.

Social Opportunities

Create opportunities for neurodivergent children to engage in social activities with peers (others with similar life challenges) as well as with younger children and adults. Neurodivergent children's deficiency in social-emotional reciprocity manifests in their difficulty in responding appropriately to others' emotions, which is one reason they may struggle to make friends or feel like they belong. Participating in events with neurotypical children is sometimes appropriate, and youth leaders should strive to create opportunities for engagement. Additionally, playing, speaking, and learning with other children "like them" could encourage a sense of belonging. They may not correctly process social cues like gestures and facial expressions, making engaging in conversations with neurotypical children challenging. Additionally, congregations can create opportunities for neurodivergent children to be involved with meaningful aspects of the worship experience. Learn their interests, goals, and areas of expertise. You may find that many neurodivergent children are subject matter experts in things they are interested in and can provide beneficial ministry to the congregation.

Learning Opportunities

Avoid trying to make neurodivergent children feel "normal" because of their disability. They are normal children whose brains process information differently than neurotypical children. An analogy is like comparing an Android smartphone to an iPhone. Both cell phones can run the same applications, but each has a different operating system. In their journal article "Category Learning in Autism: Are Some Situations Better Than Others?" researchers evaluated how school-age children with autism learned compared to neurotypical school-aged children in four different teaching situations.[8] The study revealed that autistic children were advantaged by simultaneously presenting information, while typical children were advantaged by high-intensity feedback when learning. This study is relevant because it brings awareness to the need for Christian educators and church leaders to diversify teaching methodologies that could benefit neurodivergent children. Including drama presentations or skits or showing relevant video clips during a teaching session are a few creative ideas for teachers to enhance the learning experience. Because not everyone responds to formal learning environments, additional ideas could include hosting events like karaoke sing-alongs, line dancing, and board game night, where relationships can be fostered and opportunities for faith development can occur.

Partnership Opportunities

Congregations and communities of faith can develop partnerships with nonprofit organizations and subject matter experts who specialize in neurodivergent support systems to provide education and training on neurodivergence to youth workers, greeters and ushers, and church leadership. Learning to recognize the character traits of neurodivergence can assist church leadership in being more intentional when interacting and when planning events, services, and Christian education programs. One study evaluated how effective parents of children with a learning disability would be in implementing naturalistic interventions when providing web-based coaching and training.[9] The study revealed that children communicated better when their parents had received web-based training on naturalistic intervention. Including resources in annual budgets to offer neurodiversity training educates the congregation, benefits neurodivergent children, and could be an excellent outreach opportunity.

Caregiver Opportunities

Offer a few hours of childcare service for parents or caregivers of autistic children (also a great way to express care for parents/caregivers in general) so they can enjoy some personal time. Parents of adults with autism often advocate for themselves when locating services to benefit their loved ones. Additionally, parents of neurodivergent children experience their own stresses, which affects their quality of life. In a recent study, researchers compared stress levels of parents who have children with developmental disabilities with those who do not.[10] The study surveyed 167 parents of children with developmental disabilities and 103 parents of children with no disabilities. The study concluded that parents of persons with learning disabilities implement coping strategies and often do not seek emotional support. The lack of ministry to parents and caregivers of neurodivergent children is a ministry gap that congregations can fill with minimal effort and resources.

Conclusion

Congregations and communities of faith can support families with autistic children to help them grow deeper in their faith. Awareness of the daily challenges could help church leaders and youth workers be more attentive to their needs and develop programs and strategies to accommodate them.

A ministry of this magnitude only happens with intentionality, creativity, consistency, and commitment. Neurodivergent individuals are beloved children of God, created in God's image. To be the body of Christ as we are intended to be, the church must attend to and welcome the gifts of neurodivergence in our midst.

Questions for Discussion

1. Did anything in the chapter surprise you? Does your faith community consider the social and learning needs of neurodivergent children?
2. If you have not included or considered neurodivergent children in your planning, what do you need to do so?
3. How does your faith community support all families, including families with children who are neurodivergent?

Notes

1. *The Merriam-Webster Dictionary*, rev. ed. (Springfield, MA: Merriam-Webster 2022).
2. *APA Dictionary of Psychology*, American Psychological Association, 2022, https://dictionary.apa.org/autism.
3. *APA Dictionary of Psychology*.
4. Barbara J. Newman, *Autism and Your Church: Nurturing the Spiritual Growth of People with Autism Spectrum Disorder* (Grand Rapids, MI: Friendship Ministries, 2011).
5. Robert C. Schnase, *Five Practices of Fruitful Congregations* (Nashville: Abingdon, 2018).
6. *Diagnostic and Statistical Manual of Mental Disorders*, 5th ed. (Arlington, VA: American Psychiatric Association, 2013).
7. Lynn Kern Koegel et al., "Improving Empathic Communication Skills in Adults with Autism Spectrum Disorder," *Journal of Autism and Developmental Disorders* 46, no. 3 (March 2016), 921–33, https://doi.org/10.1007/s10803-015-2633-0.
8. Anne-Marie Nader et al., "Category Learning in Autism: Are Some Situations Better Than Others?" *Journal of Experimental Psychology: General*, September 16, 2021, https://doi.org/10.1037/xge0001092.
9. Hedda Meadan et al., "Internet-Based Parent-Implemented Intervention for Young Children with Autism: A Pilot Study," *Journal of Early Intervention* 38, no. 1 (March 18, 2016): 3–23, https://doi.org/10.1177/1053815116630327.

10. Anna Bujnowska et al., "Coping with Stress in Parents of Children with Developmental Disabilities," *International Journal of Clinical and Health Psychology* 21, no. 3 (2021): 100254.

References

APA Dictionary of Psychology. American Psychological Association. 2022. https://dictionary.apa.org/autism.

"Autism Spectrum Disorder." Centers for Disease Control and Prevention. November 25, 2024. https://www.cdc.gov/autism/about/?CDC_AAref_Val=https://www.cdc.gov/ncbddd/autism/facts.html.

"Autism Spectrum Disorder." National Institute of Mental Health. Accessed December 31, 2024. https://www.nimh.nih.gov.

"Autism Spectrum Disorders." World Health Organization. Accessed December 31, 2024, https://www.who.int.

Bujnowska, Anna, Celestino Rodríguez, Trinidad García, Débora Areces, and Nigel Marsh. "Coping with Stress in Parents of Children with Developmental Disabilities." *International Journal of Clinical and Health Psychology* 21, no. 3 (2021): 100254.

Diagnostic and Statistical Manual of Mental Disorders. 5th ed. Arlington, VA: American Psychiatric Association, 2013.

Janssen, Denise. *Reclaimed: Faith in an Emerging Generation.* Valley Forge, PA: Judson, 2015.

Kern Koegel, Lynn, Kristen Ashbaugh, Anahita Navab, and Robert Koegel. "Improving Empathic Communication Skills in Adults with Autism Spectrum Disorder." *Journal of Autism and Developmental Disorders* 46, no. 3 (March 2016), 921–33. https://doi.org/10.1007/s10803-015-2633-0.

Lee, Amy Fenton. *Leading a Special Needs Ministry.* Nashville: B&H, 2016.

Lucas, Timothy D. "Creating a Social Ministry for Adults with Autism: A Model for Unity Baptist Church." PhD diss., Virginia Union University, 2024.ProQuest (3056899471).

Macaskill, Grant. "The Bible, Autism, and Other Profound Developmental Conditions: Regulating Hermeneutics." *Journal of Disability and Religion* (February 8, 2021): 1–25. https://doi.org/10.1080/23312521.2021.1881024.

Meadan, Hedda, Melinda R. Snodgrass, Lori E. Meyer, Kim W. Fisher, Moon Y. Chung, James W. Halle. "Internet-Based Parent-Implemented Intervention for Young Children with Autism: A Pilot Study." *Journal of Early Intervention* 38, no. 1 (March 18, 2016): 3–23. https://doi.org/10.1177/1053815116630327.

Meeks, Wayne A., and Jouette M. Bassle. *HarperCollins Study Bible: New Revised Standard Version, with the Apocryphal/Deuterocanonical Books.* New York: HarperCollins, 1993.

The Merriam-Webster Dictionary, Rev. ed. Springfield, MA: Merriam-Webster, 2022.

Nader, Anne-Marie, Domenico Tullo, Valérie Bouchard, Janie Degré-Pelletier, Armando Bertone, Michelle Dawson, and Isabelle Soulières. "Category Learning in Autism: Are Some Situations Better Than Others?" *Journal of Experimental Psychology: General,* September 16, 2021. https://doi.org/10.1037/xge0001092.

Newman, Barbara J. *Autism and Your Church: Nurturing the Spiritual Growth of People with Autism Spectrum Disorder.* Grand Rapids, MI: Friendship Ministries, 2011.

Schnase, Robert C. *Five Practices of Fruitful Congregations.* Nashville: Abingdon, 2018.

Afterword: Growing Together

PATRICK B. REYES

For parents, caregivers, teachers, and educators, no single activity will demand our time and attention more than raising future generations. And yet there is no other single activity about which we receive so little formal training or education. What this leads to is a fundamental gap in how future generations are nurtured, educated, and raised.

Adults raise future generations the way they were raised. By divine accident of birth if you are lucky, this is amazing. You are seen. You are loved. You are valued. You have everything this book says a child should have.

If you are unlucky, you bring the trauma of childhood with you into adulthood.

Are we willing to continue to leave this up to chance?

Unintentional raising means young people are limited by an adult's ability to assume this responsibility well and to read the signs of the times in which they are living. It is not just about being faithful as if the lives of our beloveds do not take place in a context. The rhythms of the blocks we grow up on, the shine from streetlights or blue lights from screens, or for those lucky enough like my children to be raised under stars, the divine comedy played by one's peers are the conditions that raise our young people alongside the efforts of elders.

The Ramsey, Junker, Hwang, and Fears chapters all point out this reality of raising future generations in the throes of COVID-19, trauma, immigration, and racism. Young Brown's chapter most directly addresses this reality when she writes about what to do with intergenerational trauma. What do we do to break cycles of social and interpersonal trauma? What does it mean to be a cycle breaker? What would it mean to be cycle makers?

We theorize about what good parenting is because researchers have no greater barrier than trying to research children's experience of parenting, for good, ethical reasons related to safety and past violence against children of color. Children need to consent. And we need to understand their lives. Raising children is multidirectional; children raise us. We grow together, as the title of this book implies. That is to say nothing of us who were of the latchkey kid era who were raised on *Sesame Street* and *Mr. Rogers* and had more autonomy to roam the neighborhoods than today's kids. We both raised ourselves and had a village looking after us. Gathje offers an insight here framing the roles of a parent in response to this: love and listening.

This volume asks more of us and gestures to something that has yet to be written. At the beginning of the pandemic, I was serving on the board of my child's Title I school. The school's population was a majority of students of color. I walked into a meeting, and the first question asked was, "What do we do with children who are online, and we know they are home alone?" The school taught students from kindergarten to second grade. A wealthy, white parent with advanced degrees who also served on the board immediately said, "Call CPS." I offered, "Or we can reach out to the parent, and invite them to be part of our pod or create new pods." *Growing Together: Insights and Practices for Raising Faithful Kids* offers another way to see the challenges of the day. They invite us to see that children are not private property, nor are they simply future adults in need of our protection. Instead, the authors offer an alternative—children are beloved as they are, only desiring our love and to know the love of God.

Growing Together does the work of reinforcing the belovedness of children, but I will take this opportunity to say explicitly what the chapters here left implicit. To raise faithful children, we need to *talk about the stuff parents do not want to talk about,* especially in faith communities. A book about Christian parenting needs to include ample discussion about the hard things, and I would like to invite us into conversation about some of those hard things with this afterword. I have named a few below and have given my insight as both a parent, researcher, and religious educator. The point is not to convince you that this is right, but that too often when it comes to parenting, we have taken the hard issues off the table. I have aligned these tough conversations with insights from the book itself, to make explicit what might otherwise be implicit or tacit. Christian educator Maria Harris, whose writings lift up the explicit, implicit, and null curriculum, is a gift that keeps giving to us many years later!

Children are not private property. Children are not private property and do not belong to their parents. Though much of our traditions and society treat them as such, laws and norms have made it so that parents have privatized the responsibility of children. If we are raising faithful kids, too often this means only our children. As Christians, we should be imagining *all children* are God's children. God's children are words too easily tossed around. If they are God's, they are also our children. This is a no-brainer from my Chicano, Indigenous, and even Mediterranean cultural roots, and I suspect ideas of being raised by a village can be found across many communities and cultures. It is time we started taking this seriously in America and especially in our faith communities. Have the hard discussions *about* parenting and raising children and have them often. We are raising children. I am not just raising my own.

Let us start with one topic I do not find controversial but seems to make every faith leader and community member uncomfortable when I bring it up.

Spanking and hitting a child is not faithful parenting. When you strike a child, you strike their soul. This needs to be talked about in every faith community. For parents and educators influenced by the writings of Paulo Freire, as in Junker's chapter, we often forget that one of his major works in faith communities was teaching parents that spanking and swatting children is not good parenting. Let me repeat that—especially for those communities and parents who believe it is faithful often quoting "rod" scripture—hitting a child on any part of their body is abuse. For Christians, Jesus said, "Let the children come, do not hinder them." Hitting or spanking a child is a traumatic event. It causes harm and hinders their ability to see and experience love. There are better ways to raise children, and some are offered in this book. The Wasoian and Young chapters are helpful here, but by moving past this important issue as if it is a matter already resolved, we leave room for bad theologies of child raising to continue in our homes and faith communities.

Sexual abuse. What we know from the Centers for Disease Control statistics show that one in every four girls is sexually abused, and the majority of them are abused by close family members or someone the family knew and trusted.[1] One in four. One in anything is too many children having their childhood cut off and ended early. Raising faithful children is also about giving them the full freedom of childhood. Faithful parenting is about having the courage to talk among caregivers about how to create safe pathways to adulthood. For me, not addressing abuse explicitly increases the likelihood of abuse continuing to happen among us. Conley gets us closer in her conversation about sexuality, but abuse needs to be part of the discussion, especially when abuse continues to happen in faith communities and households.

Guns. Guns are taking the lives of young people. Guns are a single-purpose machine. I have a close family member who is "grand" like what is described in Snorton's beautiful chapter exploring the role of grandparents. Anyone familiar with my story knows that I have seen and buried too many young people due to violence. The grand in my family made the case that the gun was an heirloom. Rather than debate on those terms, I asked them to talk to my children—not explain to them their political views on guns, but to tell them why this gun is so important to them. The grand told meaningful and moving stories about being in the desert with their father and church group, shooting small game—squirrels, rabbits, small birds, etc. My daughter began to cry. "Why are you crying?" he asked. "You killed all those animals. They had families. They dream." My daughter, through her tears, named a reality he did not see in himself, which was that he used an instrument of death as it was designed to be used. It is not just this emotional tie or to think about guns as part of those cultures that still see hunting as part of their purpose. For the record, I come from one such community. It is about recognizing that guns are killing our young people. We can end gun violence, and it would be faithful to do so. To borrow from the Talmud, to save a life is to save the world. To save a child's life is to make room for their descendants. This is part of raising our children without the fear of gun violence. To be faithful is to listen to young people who are crying out for adults to end gun violence.

Faith formation is a journey, not a destination, and I am being literal here. I am writing about necessary physical journeys across geography and culture. Parents cannot control the outcomes, and yet, the work does matter as Janssen and Davis both point out in their chapters. How much effort you place in your faith formation can be directly translated to your children. Do they see you active in your faith? Do you have a strong spiritual and religious practice? Lisa Miller's research published in *The Spiritual Child* reinforced the role of spiritual communities as extensions of our home families.[2] But I want to offer nuance here. She does not mean a specific creed, doctrine, or denominational affiliation. On Sunday, we look more like racial and ethnic cultural groups retreating to our zones of comfort and xenophobia. Again, Hwang's chapter is helpful for us to see the impact of this on immigrant children. Faith formation as a journey requires movement beyond our denominational and doctrinal subdivisions. Sunday remains the most divided racially and generationally (generationally when we send our children out of the sanctuary). And yet so many of us opt to stay comfortable, raising children in the comfort of those who look and sound like us. Where are the bold and courageous Christians who are opting for a *new heaven and new earth*? The journey is not just one to faithful adulthood. The journey is material and physical, where we journey to other houses of worship and communities, expanding our children's sense of belonging to the *body of I*.

There are starving and poor children and they are our children. Every day my children go to public schools and receive additional support because both have disabilities. I want to thank Lucas for the chapter on neurodivergence and disability, an understudied and often overlooked group of children in faith communities. At both my children's school and faith community, their needs are met because of fierce advocacy. What if we made that part of our faithfulness to talk about what I did as well? At my children's schools and faith communities, we talk about income disparity—a conversation I push, not because I want to make rich and poor parents uncomfortable. Rather, as a child who grew up in poverty, I know how uncomfortable it felt in my body to know the difference between myself and my classmates at lunch hour. Whether it was having to take the tray for those who needed the free lunch or opening the lunch box to find nothing but a piece of toast inside, the lunch hour is when this difference is felt by children. And children know and feel the difference. The amazing thing is young children, when they are made aware that their friends do not have the same access to wealth, food, or opportunities, they share! There is no debate or question. They have an immediate reaction to share. Raising faithful kids is about raising adults not to lose those faithful practices: I fed those who were hungry and instructed us to invite the poor to every banquet. The lunch hour is our daily banquet. Children would raise faithful adults if we watched how they share their food in public.

Politics must be talked about at the table. The number of conversations about Christian Nationalism that do not include children, young people, or the raising of them is alarming. The political is theological, and politics directly impacts the way we raise children. From the Child Tax Credit to funding for allocations for public schools and public children's programming, the political conversations others are having about your children are based on theological, faith, and values-based views. Children learn from and in many cases inherit those views. In both the "Sticky Stuff" and "Search for Freedom" sections, the political is mentioned by the authors, but I want to push this a step further to urge that children need to be included in conversations about politics in meaningful ways. To summarize the late Rubem Alves in his work *Tomorrow's Child*, a child's imagination begins with the resurrection; adults' imagination begins with the cross.[3] So too are our politics. Children can imagine a world where there is an abundance, where resurrection is possible for all people and society. Adults can imagine an instrument of torture, a state that has power over people—the rule of law. Children would not vote for the war machine, but they would invest in better parks, libraries, and schools. The political is theological, and children should be included fully in both.

Chosen Family. It is always curious to me that Christians who believe that in Jesus there is a new identity, who can quote chapter and verse, cannot fathom that the next generation would find their communities beyond their birth family or that the nuclear family is not the only way to experience family. Consider the statement, "The family structure is changing." This popular belief is not just wrong but historically inaccurate. What now constitutes a family has only been this way for a very short period in our history. For most of human history, clans, bands, tribes, groups, extended family, and cultures have been the defining structure of family. Leave it to the Chicano to write about how I have *primos* and *primas carnal* (blood) and *brothers and sisters* with whom I have exactly zero drops of blood relation. Many of us are raised in intergenerational households where aunties and uncles, grandmas, the *abuelas* on the block, and church mothers and fathers are those raising us. I want to also affirm those parents and caregivers who have had traumatic childhoods and adulthoods in their family structures; it is healthy to create boundaries for yourself and your children. You can leave your birth family or chosen family. You can choose a different family structure—one centered on love.

Cultivate Curiosity. In the effort to raise children, instruction and correction often take over. Each year, children are given more knowledge and answers as they get closer to adulthood. And each year that passes, their once expansive imagination and capacity for dreaming and questioning is diminished. Rather than see raising children to adulthood as our task, what if cultivating curiosity about their faith was? Fewer answers, more questions; fewer facts, more dreams. Sunday school is a time when we are teaching about the resurrection, talking to ancestors Moses and Elijah, when Jacob dreams, cousin Daniel hangs with lions, and mother Miriam dances to freedom. Sunday is a time when we hear about how Mary and Elizabeth are blessed with children kicking in the womb, and we wonder if we did that as well. Brother Thomas needs to touch the wounds because he does not believe what is before his eyes. He saw his friend murdered, and yet, right here, he sees him again. We get to hear about ancestor Hagar naming God, the first time a human does that, and we learn that the women find an empty tomb and are the first to name the resurrection. If there is ever a time to lean into the curiosity of a child, it is Sunday.

Growing Together is an important resource for caregivers, parents, communities, and religious educators alike. As you have read the chapters, I hope you have taken the topics presented within and the topics you are passionate about seriously. Each chapter presents itself as a new opportunity to address the fundamentals of parenting and exploring faith with children. Take nothing you care about off the table. Our children's futures, and the future of our faith communities, depend on it. Lean into your curiosity. Most importantly, remember this book is just a bunch of adults talking to each other and to you. The most important conversation is between you and a child. That conversation, more than any resource, will get you closer to raising faithful kids and growing together in that journey.

—Rev. Patrick B. Reyes, Ph.D.,
Auburn Theological Seminary

Notes

1. See "About Child Abuse," Center for Disease Control, https://www.cdc.gov/child-abuse-neglect/about/about-child-sexual-abuse.html.
2. Lisa Miller, *The Spiritual Child: The New Science for Parenting for Health and Lifelong Thriving* (New York: Picador St. Martin's Press, 2015).
3. Rubem A. Alves, *Tomorrow's Child: Imagination, Creativity, and the Rebirth of Culture* (Eugene, OR: Wipf and Stock, 1972).

Biographical Snapshots of the Contributors of Reflections in this Book

Débora B. Agra Junker is an Associate Professor of Critical Pedagogies at Garrett-Evangelical Seminary. Since 2016, she has served as founder and director of the Cátedra Paulo Freire, where she focuses on promoting Freire's contributions to religious studies. Junker's research interests include Freire's critical pedagogy, Vygotsky's cultural-historical theory, intercultural and decolonial studies, as well as liberation theologies.

Margaret L. Conley, LCSW, MDiv, is the Executive Director of MLC Consulting LLC and the President of Mending Life Concepts Empowerment Group, Inc. Margaret is a Licensed Clinical Social Worker. She is trained as a trauma therapist. Margaret is a Certified Daring Way™ Facilitator and LEGO® Serious Play® Facilitator. Margaret is a Certified Mental Health First Aid Instructor endorsed by the National Council for Mental Wellbeing. Margaret believes that if we can harmonize our emotions, we can experience wholeness as we mend life together.

Dr. Carmichael D. Crutchfield is the Vice President of Academic Affairs/Dean and Professor of Christian Education, Spiritual Formation and Youth Ministry at Memphis Theological Seminary. He also serves as the General Secretary of the Department of Christian Education and Formation of the Christian Methodist Episcopal Church.

Dr. Russell W. Dalton is a Professor of Religious Education and Coordinator for Vocation Development at Brite Divinity

School on the campus of Texas Christian University in Fort Worth, Texas. His publications include *Children's Bibles in America: A Reception History of the Story of Noah in US Children's Bibles; Marvelous Myths: Marvel Superheroes and Everyday Faith; Faith Journey through Fantasy Lands: A Christian Dialogue with Harry Potter; Star Wars and The Lord of the Rings;* and *Video, Kids, and Christian Education*. Dr. Dalton has led national and regional conferences on topics related to children and the Bible, children's Bibles, preparing congregations to engage in acts of justice, and religion and popular culture.

Zanique Davis is a wife to her soulmate, Zamar, and a dynamic mother to her amazing boys, Zayn and Zayd. She is an ordained Itinerant Elder in the African Methodist Episcopal Church committed to shepherding, discipling, and enhancing the Christian formation of diverse groups. Zanique is an educator who enjoys teaching in the church or corporate spaces. She is currently enrolled in the PhD program in Christian Education at Garrett-Evangelical Theological Seminary.

Mary Leslie Dawson-Ramsey is an ordained deacon in the Tennessee-Western Kentucky Annual Conference of the United Methodist Church. She has served as a Christian Educator, Program Minister, and teacher of science and outdoor education congregations, communities, and schools in Atlanta, Georgia; Clarksville, Tennessee; and Memphis, Tennessee. She is passionate about connecting Christian faith and environmental sustainability.

Rev. Barbara Annette Fears, PhD, is an Associate Professor of Religious Education at Howard University School of Divinity, where she teaches courses in the history, theory, and practice of ministry. Her research focuses on matters of power, privilege and accountability in spiritual formation, praxis of faith, and curriculum development. She works with local denominations to develop curriculum and is ordained clergy in the United Church of Christ.

Dr. Peter Gathje is chair of the Fine Arts and Humanities Division at LeMoyne-Owen College in Memphis, Tennessee. He is an ethicist who has taught at various colleges and seminaries. He lives in Memphis with his wife and elementary-age daughter.

Heesung Hwang is an Associate Professor of United Methodist Studies, Christian Education, and Leadership at the Pacific School of Religion in Berkeley, California. She is also an ordained deacon in the United Methodist Church. She is the author of *Reframing Christian Education for a Global Generation*.

Rev. Dr. Denise Janssen is a scholar, author, and academic leader presently serving as Associate Research Professor of Christian Education and Assistant Dean for Academics at the Samuel DeWitt Proctor School of Theology at Virginia Union University. She has published in the areas of youth ministry, curriculum development, racial justice, and Christian education. She lives in Richmond, Virginia, with her spouse, Rev. Randy Creath.

Teresa E. Jefferson-Snorton is the Ecumenical Bishop and Program Development Officer for the Christian Methodist Episcopal Church. She is the Program Administrator for the denomination's Reimagining Children's Ministry project. She has extensive experience as a theological educator, a board-certified chaplain and ACPE Educator, and a leader of faith-based nonprofit organizations and boards.

Rev. Dr. Virginia A. Lee is the Associate Professor of Christian Education, Director of Deacon Studies, and Director of the Master of Arts in Faith, Culture, and Educational

Leadership at Garrett-Evangelical Theological Seminary in Evanston, Illinois. Her primary teaching revolves around child advocacy and centering the voices and experiences of children. She enjoys reading, crocheting, walking, and playing with and learning from her ten great-nieces/nephews.

Dr. Timothy Lucas, DMin, is a multifaceted professional with extensive experience in ministry and program management, including military, government, and nonprofit sectors. A licensed and ordained pastor with over thirty years of experience, he is passionate about helping churches develop ministries to support autistic adults and their caregivers. He resides in Huntsville, Alabama, with his wife of over thirty-three years, Rochelle Lucas.

Rev. Dr. Emily A. Peck is a Visiting Professor of Christian Formation and Young Adult Ministry at Wesley Theological Seminary in Washington, DC. She lives in Maryland with her three children, who keep her on her toes, and their dog, who has ginormous ears.

G. Lee Ramsey Jr. is an ordained elder in the Tennessee-Western Kentucky Annual Conference of the United Methodist Church. After serving congregations in Georgia and Tennessee, he taught for twenty-five years at Memphis Theological Seminary in the areas of pastoral care and preaching. Both recently retired, Lee and Mary Leslie enjoy spending lots of time with their two young grandchildren and gardening together.

Rev. Patrick B. Reyes, PhD, is an award-winning Chicano writer. He serves as the dean of Auburn Theological Seminary and provides leadership on many boards in theological and higher education. He is a "pa" to his two children, Ash and Carmelita, and lives and writes from ancestral lands in the Southwest.

Rev. Dr. Tamar Wasoian is an independent scholar, religious educator, and a teaching elder in the Presbyterian Church (U.S.A). She is Associate Pastor and Program Director at common cathedral, which is an outdoor church for the unhoused in Boston. Storied learning and urban ministries are at the core of Dr. Wasoian's interests and expertise. She loves children and has worked with them in diverse contexts and cultures.

Rev. Mary H. Young, EdD, is a recently retired administrator with the Association of Theological Schools in the United States and Canada. She has spent her career as an educator, pastor, and denominational leader. Dr. Young lives in North Chesterfield, Virginia, and currently consults with churches and educational institutions.

Dr. Jessica Young Brown is a Licensed Clinical Psychologist and Assistant Professor of Psychology at Virginia Commonwealth University. Her primary interest is in how faith and mental health intersect. She is a mom of two and a lover of belly laughs, kettle corn, and autumn afternoons.